# One Must Also Be Hungarian

ONE MUST ALSO BE

# Hungarian

**ADAM BIRO**

TRANSLATED BY

**Catherine Tihanyi**

THE UNIVERSITY OF CHICAGO PRESS

CHICAGO AND LONDON

ADAM BIRO is founder and owner of the art book publishing house Biro Éditeur. He is the author of eight previous books, including *Two Jews on a Train*, also published by the University of Chicago Press. CATHERINE TIHANYI is a translator and research associate at Western Washington University.

The University of Chicago Press, Chicago 60637
The University of Chicago Press, Ltd., London
© 2006 by The University of Chicago
All rights reserved. Published 2006
Printed in the United States of America

15 14 13 12 11 10 09 08 07 06     1 2 3 4 5

ISBN-13: 978-0-226-05212-0 (cloth)
ISBN-10: 0-226-05212-5 (cloth)

Originally published as *Les Ancêtres d'Ulysse* © 2002
by Presses Universitaires de France.

Library of Congress Cataloging-in-Publication Data
Biro, Adam
[Ancêtres d'Ulysse. English]
One must also be Hungarian / Adam Biro ; translated by Catherine Tihanyi.
    p.  cm.
Originally published in 2002 as Les Ancêtres d'Ulysse.
ISBN 0-226-05212-5 (cloth : alk. paper)
1. Biro, Adam—Family.  2. Authors, French—20th century—Family relationships.
3. Jews—Hungary—Biography.  I. Tihanyi, Catherine.  II. Title.
PQ2662.I733Z46413 2006
843'.914—dc22                                           2006014149
[B]

*I am telling the history of the Greeks.*
*I am telling all that I know. What I don't know*
                    *I am inventing. The tale often tells the truth.*

XENOS OF SEPHER

# Contents

## TRANSLATOR'S NOTE AND ACKNOWLEDGMENTS

This translation includes an additional introduction for English-speaking readers. The author has also taken this opportunity to make some minor changes in the original text itself so that the English text is at variance with the French edition in some places.

My heartfelt thanks to Adam Biro for his patience in answering all translation questions and his thorough review of the final English text. I would also like to thank T. David Brent for entrusting me with this translation and for his helpful suggestions and comments, Mara Naselli for her fine manuscript editing and suggestions, and Martin Schwab for reading the manuscript translation for the University of Chicago Press and contributing a number of insightful remarks.

# Introduction
## to the English Edition

I had two reasons for writing this book. The first is my love of writing. Although I earn my living as an art book publisher, an endeavor taking up the better part of my time, writing remains for me an inexhaustible source of happiness.

The second reason for undertaking this reflection on my family's history was my father's death. His passing meant the end of an old Hungarian family in Hungary, a Jewish and Hungarian family, that is, a Jewish but Hungarian family—my own family. Its history is now continuing elsewhere, in France where I live, and where my two daughters and my grandson Ulysse were born. Thus, at this historical moment, I wanted to take stock and put down for Ulysse and future generations what I knew about my family as it had been, then and over there. I wanted to tell the story of a world and a time now gone.

But my need for literature kept me from doing research and transforming this writing project into a scholarly work of history. I felt that it was unnecessary, and particularly that it was not my place to tell the history of Hungary, to give the location of the Tisza, to study the relations between Romanians and Hungarians . . .

But I was wrong. I cannot expect the American reader to know more about the great Hungarian plain or Transylvania than I know about Milwaukee or Nebraska. My publisher thus convinced me to provide keys to help make the book understandable on the other side of the Atlantic.

Allow me to tell two stories that give a clearer view of Hungary than any sociohistorical study could. The White House adviser for Eastern Europe asks to see President Franklin D. Roosevelt in 1942.

"Mr. President," the adviser announces, "the kingdom of Hungary has declared war on us."

"Who is the present king of Hungary?"

"This kingdom doesn't have a king. It is ruled by a rear admiral."

"Mm . . . a rear admiral . . . How strong is the Hungarian navy?"

"There's no navy. Hungary has no sea."

"Wars are often waged for religious reasons. So what is the main religion there?"

"Catholicism."

"So this Catholic rear admiral . . ."

"He is Protestant, Mr. President."

"So I assume since Hungary has declared war on us it has some territorial claims against the United States?"
The adviser replies, "It has none."

"So, it must have some against one of our allies, the Soviet Union, England . . ."

"None either."

"So, against whom?" asks Roosevelt.

"Against Romania," says the advisor.

"So Hungary has declared war on Romania?"

"No, Mr. President. Romania and Hungary are allies."

This gives an idea of the complexity of the country that was mine, located as it is in the heart of Europe, between the Germans and the Slavs.

So what is it that we should know? The Hungarians (they call themselves Magyars) are not Slavic. They settled down in their present country in the Carpathian basin during the ninth century. They came from central Asia, from the shores of the Caspian Sea. In spite of their name, they are not the descendants of Attila's Huns. They speak a language thought to be difficult because it is not Indo-European. Hungarian along with Finnish and Estonian (and some Siberian languages) make up the Finno-Ugric language family, and along with Basque, which defies classification, are the only European languages that do not belong to the Indo-European group. The Hungarian people, only ten million strong, created an extraordinary literature with their language that is so rich, expressive, and melodious. Hungary has produced an abundant number of great musicians equal to that of its great poets. In a different domain, Hungarians played a prominent role in the creation of Hollywood, the main vehicle of American myths. Names such as Korda, Cukor, Curtiz, de Toth, Lengyel, Molnar readily come to mind—and then of course the Bartok sisters and Zsa Zsa Gabor, and Tony Curtis, and let's not forget Bela Lugosi in his infamous role of Dracula, the Transylvanian prince (Transylvania is my homeland).

The story goes that there was the following sign above the door of a Hollywood studio: "It's not enough to be Hungarian to make films. One must also have talent." Capra is said to have turned this phrase around: "It's not enough to have talent to make films. One must also be Hungarian." Hungarians also hold a prominent place among the great photographers of the twentieth century, foremost among them: Brassaï, Kertész, Moholy-Nagy, Munkacsi, Capa. Vitamin C was discovered by the Nobel prize winner Albert Szentgyörgyi, and there were two Hungarians, Teller and Szilard, among the fathers of the American atomic bomb. And of course, who hasn't heard of George Soros, or of Theodor Herzl, the founder of the state of Israel, who was born in Budapest, on the very spot of the great synagogue? And of course we had Béla Bartok, Zoltán Kodály, George Solti, and Eugene Ormandy.

Hungary was independent till 1526 and then was occupied successively by Turks, Austrians (for four hundred years), Germans (at the end of World War II) and finally by the Soviet Union (from 1945 to 1989). It picked the wrong side in both world wars and thus lost both. It lost two-thirds of its territory in the treaty of Trianon in 1919. It also picked the wrong political regimes: feudalism till 1918, a right-wing semidictatorial regime till World War II, the Nazi terror at the end of the war, a bloody Communist regime till the Revolution of 1956, and then a more tempered one till the fall of the regime.

Hungarian history is tragic. And so, here is the second story. A Hungarian, unprepared for the Chicago cold, goes to a shop to buy a scarf. He chooses the least expensive one, and when it is time to pay for it, he realizes that he left his wallet at the hotel and has only Hungarian currency, forints, in his pockets. The shopkeeper will only accept dollars. He is really sorry so he offers to save the scarf till his customer comes back with American money. But the shopkeeper can't help being curious and asks to see the forints. He has never seen any and doesn't know if he will ever again have the opportunity to see what they look like. The Hungarian shows him the first bill featuring the portrait of a proud man wearing a big moustache and a fur hat.

"This is Rákóczi, a Transylvanian prince. In the seventeenth century he led a revolt against the Habsburgs who were then ruling Hungary and Transylvania."

"Did he succeed?"

"Not in the least. His army was crushed and he died in exile in Turkey."

"Ouch! How about this other guy with the beard?"

"That's Count Széchenyi István, a moderate nineteenth-century revolutionary. The Habsburgs had him thrown in prison. He died insane in a mental asylum in Austria—though it is suspected he was murdered."

"Gosh, this is horrible! And what about this youngish one?"

The customer gets excited: "Ah, this is Petöfi Sándor, the greatest Hungarian poet of the nineteenth century . . ."

"And why is he depicted so young?"

"Because he died at age twenty-six, killed on the battlefield. His body was never found."

"But this is all so horrible. And who is this last one, looking so ferocious?"

"That's the twenty-forint bill with Dózsa György, the leader of a peasant rebellion at the beginning of the sixteenth century whom the nobles had burnt alive on a burning throne. His companions were forced to eat pieces of his flesh."

The Chicago shopkeeper thought a moment before exclaiming, "Good grief! You poor man! Put these horrible bills back in your pocket, take this scarf and get out of here. I don't ever want to see any of these bills again!"

Today Hungary is a poor country. It isn't easy for it to enter the twenty-first century but since the fall of the communist regime it has become a member of NATO and on May 1, 2004, it joined the European Union. Will the country be able to bring up wages and pensions to the European level, rather than just prices? Will it be able to do away with the new inequalities created by the change of regime and the advent of the market economy? Will it be able to stem the tide of xenophobia and anti-Semitism that now openly reaches up to the parliament? (Hatred of Jews has existed in Hungary only since the nineteenth century, or rather, Hungarians were no more anti-Semitic than other nations. However, anti-Semitism rapidly grew to major proportions and during World War II, Eichmann was able to perpetrate his harm with the support of the authorities, the police, and, it has to be said, with the indifference and often with the collaboration of the population. Hungary was also Hitler's last ally and was liberated by Soviet troops on April 4, 1945, just one month before the end of the war, while Paris was already freed in August of 1944.)

There were a million and a half Jews living in the territory of the greater Hungary before Trianon. They were mostly urban and they largely participated in the intellectual, artistic, commercial, and industrial life of the country. They were nationalist patriots who spoke only Hungarian, except for a Yiddish-speaking minority in marginal areas. This comes out again in Primo Levi's *Survival in Auschwitz*, in which he notes that, at one time, only Hungarian was heard in Auschwitz. At present, about sixty thousand Jews live in Hungary, most of them in Budapest, the capital.

The Hungarian national anthem is the only sad and desperate anthem in the world. It was written in the nineteenth century and even the communist regime kept it. Instead of the usual lyrics claiming "we are the best," "our fatherland is above all others," "we shall win against all," it states, "this nation has already suffered the price for the past and the future."

*Paris, May 2004*

# One Must Also Be Hungarian

| Családi és kereszt- vagy elő- és egyébb mellék-név | Születési év, hó és nap | |
|---|---|---|
| 1 | 2 | |
| Finkelstein Ábrahám | Január 1-én 1806. | |
| Finkelstein Sali neje született: Ichilovits | Julius 10 1848 | |
| Finkelstein Jakab fia | Május 13. 1853. | |

# 1

## Finkelstein Ábrahám

Finkelstein Ábrahám lived seven generations before Ulysse. He was thus his great-great-grandfather's great-grandfather (this is meaningless: seven generations, that's too much, and suddenly, when speaking of my own family, that ancestor feels more distant in time and unreal than the Romans or Charlemagne). As Ulysse's grandfather, I find myself near the end of the list in its present state—present because it is infinite—but my importance in it is greater than might be thought given my place. This is because I am the one telling the story—none of our ancestors decided to do this, at least as far as I know. Of course there's still the possibility that J. will have a go at it. She is only thirty years old and might yet experience the desire to become the family historian. But how would she be able to do it? I am the only one who can do it as I am the last to have known the world of Then and Over There, the place known, not too long ago, as the other side of Europe.

*This mysterious and mythical other side (of Europe) that I loved, that I have so often described in writing and even more often by speaking to an increasingly jaded audience as I kept on repeating my nostalgic expatriate refrain ... this other Europe, whose bittersweet specificity I both praised and criticized, is fast disappearing. Eastern or Central Europe (these two terms are synonymous over there just as they are over here) from where I am so proud of hailing, of originating, is no longer the source of dark geniuses like Kafka, of Hungarian suicides and musicians, of Dr. Sigmund and other Austro-Hungarian kindred spirits (Austro-Hungarian as they say, but we do know that it's either Austro or Hungarian while the two together ... unmöglich!), of towering poets like Ady, of painters gushing symbols ... This Europe has no longer any talent, no longer any creators. It has now joined the chase for the buck, and this is so sad, so lonely ...*

*(The following has nothing to do with my story but it is linked to it by subtle ties: In New York, a few years ago, I saw a superb musical, Chicago. I am very fond of musicals—I find there's a profound charm to their simplicity. I enjoy the involuntary humor of their plots and the idiocy of the dialogues; I am fond of the foot taping tunes, their lightness and their rhythm, which even someone with a wooden ear like me can recognize and even a clumsy mouth like mine can whistle years later. I am enchanted by the precision of the choreography, the perfect coordination of the dancers, the dream women who are dressed in su-*

persexy clothes, and, in addition to being sculptural beauties, have so many mind boggling talents: they and their male fellow cast members are dancers, singers, gymnasts . . . And then there the performers who are "just" dancers, they too are extraordinary! I was enchanted by Chicago, the musical; it has an abundance of all the ingredients for success. The bad guys are very bad, the good gals are very good and very innocent; there was plenty of laughter. The action was happening in a prison, a joke prison. And then, suddenly, a young woman speaks in a language totally fantastic and thus incomprehensible: it was supposed to be Hungarian. She claims her innocence—in vain. In this ultralight musical comedy in which beauty, gracefulness, lightness, and cheerfulness triumph, there is a tragic moment that is unnecessary for the scene or the plot: the Hungarian woman is hung. The same thing happens in Woody Allen's The Curse of the Jade Scorpion, in which the evil magician's name is Polgar: a Hungarian. Wherever there is doubt, trouble, the shadow of the tragic, the smell of despair—just scratch a bit, and you'll find a Hungarian . . . )

J. is one of my daughters, but despite her interest for this old Europe, her interest for my story as well as that of her mother, she wouldn't really be able to tell it the way it was because she was born HERE. This is not such a bad thing in that it is safer—her life is more secure, but it is also a bit unfortunate because, since she was born here, this means she is not from OVER THERE (as to my daughter Y., it's Africa that holds her interest). Over There is the greatest country of Europe and it will never be part of their Europe . . . the EU-nizing, Euronizing one, a Europe reduced to a market. Over There cannot become part of this Europe because it no longer exists.

I have memories of that country, of the Over There, of the oldendays. Memories that are so alive, overgrown, hypertrophied. I have the feeling that my life happened Over There, that since these fifteen years I spent in Budapest, the first fifteen years of my life, nothing im-

5

*portant has happened to me. The poems, the history of the country, its writers, its sport figures, its crooks, its singers, its politicians—all of its politicians, its sayings in Hungarian and in pig-Latin, "Quod licet Jovi, non licet bovi," "Si tacuisses, philosophus mensisses," the jokes, the subtleties of language, even the ads on the walls on the way to school ("Hey, ox, why are you so sad? Because the price of carp has gone down." "Beer is liquid bread"), the dirty puns, the counting rhymes, the places only known to me, names and people, my buddies from kindergarten and elementary school, insignificant events such as someone entering a room and saying that . . . , the other answering that . . . —"but this can't be, you can't remember this, you were only two and a half years old." "I remember it perfectly well, even that it was yellow and not very big." For heaven's sakes, why, what happened Over There for me to have memories that are so fresh, so now? Dr. Freud's explanations come up short, so do those from textbooks. "Everything happens before age six," etc. One day, a woman told me, "It's because over there you were loved." But here too, it seems to me I am loved. However, over there, I was loved unconditionally, for free. Here, love has to be earned, I have to give something in exchange for it.*

*The impossibility of communicating this Over There, of bringing it here, of making it felt . . . even to those I love and who love me . . . Volt egy szúnyog meg egy légy. Tovább is van, mondjam még? Mondjaaad! Volt egy szúnyog meg egy légy. Tovább is van, mondjam még? And so forth , until . . . death. ("There was a mosquito and a fly. It goes on, need I say it? Sayayayay! There was a mosquito and a fly. It goes on, need I say it? . . . )*

Time stretches out, yesterday is so terribly already gone. I can barely make out my childhood face of fifty years ago through the whitish fog of another century, and the boundaries become blurry. We are all reliving a vital experience, one that is unique, like no other. It is experienced anew over and over again, and our loves, our lives, our death can only be ours.

Finkelstein Ábrahám (Hungarians and their distant cousins, the Japanese, place family names before given names) was born in 1806. Where did I find this information (there's no question mark here because it's not a question—it introduces the topic at hand). Next week I have to go to Budapest to move my father's things out of his apartment because he died not too long ago, and I miss him. I will take all of the family's papers with me and I will check them to see from which Hungarian village Ábrahám originated.

*It's done. I went back to their Budapest apartment. I went there, once again, for the hundredth, the millionth, and now, once more, for the last, time. When my parents were still alive, I used to go to Budapest by train, by car, and when I finally earned a regular salary, by plane . . . and always, everyday, night and day, in my thoughts. But this time I went there to sell their apartment. My parents, newlywed in 1937, had been the first to live in this building that had just been built in a new neighborhood of the capital. The neighborhood was first populated by young middle class civil servants and intellectuals, for the most part Jewish. My parents never moved away. They were living there when I was born, and it is from there that I left fifteen years later. For me, Hungary is first of all this apartment. The furniture had been made by a cabinet maker to fit these very rooms, and they lasted up till now. I sold their apartment, their home, the only fixed point my father ever knew, the place that gave him reassurance, that made it possible for him to exist. Every time we were nearing it, after visiting someone or after a walk, he would happily say, "we are now navigating on home waters." First I emptied the apartment: gave away the* furniture and the clothes, sold or gave away the books and old optical instruments, threw away knickknacks and chipped cups, took away with me all the photographs (thousands, they filled two trunks), all the paintings (those by Józsi, my painter uncle along with the others), all the official documents, and then, once completely emptied, I sold it. I also threw away all the old suitcases that my mother had kept for the last fifty years. When the cleaning lady was doing a major spring cleaning and had wanted to put them in the trash, my mother grabbed them from her hands: "They will come in handy when we'll have to flee." The last piece of furniture that a cabinetmaker was willing to take to remodel and resell, was a long china cabinet-serving table in cherry wood that also featured a glass fronted bar. It was very modern for the times in 1937 and had electric bulbs hidden inside. During meals, dishes and cutlery were stacked on a pullout board. One day, around 1953 or 1954, I don't know through what miracle, a foreigner, a Swedish businessman came to bring us news of Józsi's wife in Stockholm. This was a miracle because, just as Hungarians were forbidden to leave Hungary, no foreigners were allowed to enter the country at that time—I had never known or even seen one. My parents invited him for dinner—it was a very formal occasion and it has remained imprinted in my memory. My grandmother Bíró and my great-uncle Nándor were also invited. The Swede gave me a British shilling; I had never even seen a foreign coin. I gazed at it for days, until my mother told me not to show it to anybody because no one had the right to have foreign money at home. I became so frightened that I slid the coin behind the pullout board of the china cabinet. But the coin fell—I heard it fall behind the board—and for years I worried that someone could find it, denounce us and that my parents would go to prison. I assume, or rather, I know that the coin is still inside that cabinet but I did not dare ask the cabinetmaker to pry it open. It would have been childish and, at age sixty, I am no longer a kid from Tátra Street even though

I still feel like one. Whether I want it or not, I have to be an adult.

I went back, just before my appointment with the future owner, to see the apartment one last time even though it was empty. This was on an eighth day of May. My father's smell was still lingering there so strongly I felt I could almost touch it. He had left these rooms seven months previously, after sixty three years of continuous presence. The new owner, a woman, arrived. She was in a happy mood and exactly thirty years younger than I. I started to tell her the history of the apartment, and then that of the building. I am the only one who knows it because all the present owners moved in long after I left. Their stories blend in with that of the country. "On May 8, 1945, I was three and a half years old. Was it morning? I can't remember but I was in bed, you see, right at this spot. It was a nice day, this window, no, no, that one, was opened, and someone, a man's voice, shouted from over there in the courtyard: 'the waaaaar is ooooover!' I remember this moment so very clearly . . ." The young woman, completely taken by her happiness of having bought this apartment for her future children, was not listening. She had no interest in me, my memories, my stories, my story. The history of the building did not interest her. She was talking about changing the layout of the apartment. The kitchen should go on the street side, the two bedrooms on the courtyard side . . . Now it is me who is no longer interested, who no longer listens.

The apartment had been lively, noisy, filled with people. My mother created LIFE there. There was constant movements, shouts, and then, long after my departure, there were the two radios set on two different channels and the TV, all sorts of people who passed through to tell something, to explain, to request, to specify, to demand, to listen, to give an account, to borrow, to beg, to cancel . . . Now a DEADLY SILENCE reigns over the apartment. It is bereft of furniture, of things, of people, it is lifeless. I have trouble comprehending this. And this silence spreads over the whole of the country, over the self that belonged *here: with my parents deaths I no longer have any close family in Hungary. My ancestors lived there for at least four centuries, but probably longer (where did they come from?)—and now, it's over, and the game will be played elsewhere, at this time in France ... and then elsewhere again. The fate of the wandering Jew, of the eternal Jew—I take it on, I claim it. But without the fault we have been accused of: I have never denied my help to any cross-bearing Jesus.*

*My parents lived here the whole of a life, a regular-folk life. Now they are dead, they no longer exist, their things no longer exist, even the place where they lived will cease to exist. What is the use of a person's life? The unbearable feeling of an unavoidable death and other such banalities, this is what I am thinking about in the May sunshine in the middle of my mother's empty room, forever emptied of my mother, of me, of me as a child, forever.*

*And those things, those objects we are so attached to, that we buy, store, clean, that we are accustomed to, that surround us, structure us ... I gave away all of my mother's clothes to a charity that took them away in the whole of twenty minutes, and I threw away the rest, including letters, mementoes, knickknacks, along with other personal possessions into a garbage can at the end of the street. In a single evening, I thus wiped out the visible traces of a life.*

Among my father's things, there were so many documents, official papers. He kept everything, birth certificates of family members, reports cards, what have you (this again does not call for a question mark). It is there that I found the ancestors' file.

This file: in 1940 or in '41, I'm not sure which, it's the fact that matters, the fact that the pieces-of-garbage goons of the government of the piece-of-garbage regent horthy (I write his name without capitalizing it, so much I hate him and I notice with pleasure that the word "garbage" already made an accidental appearance in the previous paragraph) forced Hungarian Jews to prove that they were Hungarian, that their ancestors had lived on the Hungarian territory since 1863, and this without interruption. . . . Well, my ancestors were more Hungarian than the monument of the Millennium on Heroes' Square in Budapest, near Gundel's restaurant, which has the reputation of being the best in the country. They were more Hungarian—those idiots-who-didn't-know-what-was-going-to-happen-to-them, who-couldn't-wouldn't-notice—more Hungarian than the Tisza, than the *puszta*. They were more Magyars, or rather as Magyar as the others in their behavior, their thinking and their attitude. With hindsight, from here, afterwards . . . much later, it is easy to judge, even easier to not understand. All this makes me horribly sad. Out of the six millions Jews that were exterminated, one out of ten came from this small country of around fifteen million people—so in Auschwitz, one Jew out of three had a Hungarian passport. Among my close kin, my grand-father and my uncle who were killed were not murdered by Germans but by Hungarians . . . So what can I say of this country and its people? And mostly what can I say about those people for whom Hungary was everything? I left Hungary over the opposition of my parents, mainly of my father, and he remained extremely bitter about this for the rest of his life. One of the reasons was his gut attachment to his country. I still can see him, at dawn on December 9, 1956, standing at the entrance of our apartment, in one of those striped pajamas that were only manufactured in communist bloc countries, one finger theatrically raised, reciting a verse from a famous nine-

11

teenth century patriotic hymn: "You must live and die here!"

And so my parents had to write to villages and towns to ask for their ascendants' birth and death certificates. This is how I came to discover, in this shameful and indispensable file, this day-laborer ancestor. I am as proud of him as if he were a duke. And even more so, because I have more dislike than affection for dukes. This day laborer was at the ground zero level of agricultural wage earners. He was paid at the end of each work day and didn't know whether he would be rehired for the next . . . and so on, for a whole lifetime. It was written: Finkelstein Ábrahám, born in 1806. I don't know where, this was not mentioned. Only the dates of his birth and death, and his profession: *napszámos*. Day laborer. What was his life like, this ancestor of mine—I, who was already counting up at fifty the pension I would get when I became seventy, eighty years old? I, who pays dues to the URSSAF (csg/crds T, sickness, widowhood, old age A, old age depla. T), to the ASSEDIC (asf. A, asf B, fngs T, apec cadre B, retraite cadre B) to the Agirc T, to Expar B, to the prév. cadre A and B, to the formation pro & tx apprentiss., and I am not even mentioning the others, even more obscene.[1] He must have been a pious man, of course, since they all were pious, the Jews of that time and of over there, he thus had many children, how did he bring them up? How did he dare make children without knowing how he would feed them the next day?

This is all I know of him. Day laborer. Born in 1806. Napoleon was still alive—good grief! Napoleon was still emperor while Ábrahám was day laborer. (But when they showed up

1. The author has a way of inventing acronyms, so some of these might be legitimate and some imaginary, and some again a combination of both. The meaning comes from the absurdity conveyed by the list. *Trans.*

Above, the Great Writer wrote in the Great Book: "empering-er" and "LABOROR" so as to reestablish the balance, but Ábrahám had earned the right to capital letters.) Cézanne wasn't born yet. Ábrahám couldn't imagine what his descendants were to endure, nor the name and the face and the way of being of one of his great-great-grand sons, me. He couldn't have imagined that against all mathematical probability I would be, in the year 2001, his only descendant—and his opposite in gestures, in words, in thoughts, in all of my being. That I would leave the country and that I would speak with my wife and my children another language than his. That I would eat oysters and that I would like salami and even smoked paprika sausages. That I would go to the synagogue only once a year, at Yom Kippur, like all *Yom-Kippur-yid*—atheist but ashamed. That I would make love naked, and even outside on the grass, and for the sole pleasure of it. And that I would know nothing about him, born about one hundred and fifty years before I was: except that he was a peasant, that he worked for peasants, pushing (or worse, pulling?) a plow and harvesting wheat, corn, everything. That he took care of the farm animals–not pigs, but in Hungary it would be hard to avoid. He did not own any land, had no land of his own, he owned nothing, that is certain. He was a Jewish peasant, barely a peasant, the dregs of the agricultural universe, miserable, they did exist, believe me! Yes, ladies and gents, they were not all Rothschilds. And just like him, I cannot see the face, the bearing of the grandchild who will be born from me in one hundred years. Will he be a laborer, again? An alpha-plus or a beta? How many clones will he have? And I who was a breach birth and caused horrible pain to my mother, and am now *Monsieur l'Editeur,* and

13

*Monsieur le Directeur* . . . and I was even on TV! Is this cause for tears or for laughter? (And even Ulysse, in thirty years, I can only dream it—a very fuzzy dream.) Finkelstein Ábrahám died at age fifty-three, in 1859, only nine years after having married Schilovits Sali (or Rozália), born in 1818.

Among their children, the only one of whom I know more than the name, Finkelstein Jakab, born in 1853 in Nagy-Rápold. A *Kulcsár* by profession, a sort of doorman. *Kulcs* means key. The keeper of the keys? The concierge? Was he a concierge, a super? Or what? Another version, another document, an old letter states "merchant." Of what? My mother basically told me this ancestor was a soda water seller. He was delivering seltzer water siphons on his cart to taverns around Arad, in Transylvania.

# 2

# Finkelstein Jenö

According to my mother, Finkelstein Jakab, my great-grand
father cart driver, seltzer water deliverer, was so poor that he
didn't have the luxury of raising all of his children, so that
my grandfather, born Finkelstein Jenö (keep this in mind,
because things are going to get complicated), had to be put
up for adoption.

Jenö had a brother Aladár. I knew and remember him,
even though I saw him only rarely, but I can't remember his
wife's face. Before the war, Aladár owned a shirt store in Budapest that he continued to run under the new regime till

the shop was nationalized (legally confiscated) and then Aladár was only tolerated in it as a sales clerk. Their son was deported to Auschwitz and didn't come back. (This last detail is pure Westernese. To a Hungarian reader, the first part of the sentence already contains the second part.)

And as if this death were not enough, it caused a rift in the family. This is why I can remember Aladár a little but his wife not at all. My grandmother is said to have asked her sister-in-law, shortly after the war, how she was doing. Her sister-in-law exploded in anger "We have lost our only son, but you, all your family is still alive. You are in disgustingly good health and spirits, so how dare you ask me how I'm doing." This is how I heard the story. The lady in question kept her resentment toward my grandparents till her dying days.

*You'll tell me, That's ridiculous, your grandmother didn't do anything bad, on the contrary. And yet, there is no ridicule in this. You have to understand what sort of times they lived in, what that wound was,*

*what those wounds were, that death, those deaths. You have to know*
*human history and the human soul (long laughter from the audience).*
*She was right and she was also wrong. It was better not to talk to some*
*people. Others, on the contrary, needed to be around people all the*
*time. There was no rule. At times the desire for solitude, at times the*
*need for compassion . . .*

Their son disappeared, leaving behind a child who, much later when the family's wounds had finally turned into scars, became a true friend even though he was more than ten years older than I. He was a great guy, a psychiatrist who was as well pessimist and negative, who looked upon life as absurd, and who met, while still young, a death as absurd as life: an accident in which part of a wall fell on him while he was walking his dog.

The dog disappeared with his leash, forever.

(I was told however, that my grandfather and Aladár never stopped seeing each other. They met every morning on the road to the courthouse . . . I'll come back to this later.)

My grandfather, Finkelstein Jenö, was thus adopted. I assume by a neighbor in Arad, in Transylvania where he lived, rather than in Szkrofa, his birth village in the Hunyad province in Hungary (which might as well be on the moon). But this is not important. Not only is it of no interest to the reader, but I don't care about it. The reason I am digging into this is that it seems (and is!) distant. I feel this distance and I want to share the feeling of that distance: in space and time, a bit outdated, never boring. All of this story happened in a part of the world that well-meaning readers know nothing about, and that no longer exist under the name of the configuration of that time. Transylvania. The cart driver with his siphons

. . . All just as distant and exotic as Ladakh, Patagonia, or the seventeenth century.

But wait till you learn the rest: the widow who adopted my grandfather was Catholic, and, if we are to believe the *y* at the end of her name, she was a member of the nobility (or perhaps Swiss? There are some Luy in the Valais). She was called Widow Lady Czapff Vilmos, born Luy Mária. She must have thus married a German or an Austrian. But why was my grandfather's name changed from Jenö (Eugene) to György (George) as neither one was Jewish? By now, only God knows.

But my grandfather, Finkelstein Jenö, began his long self-naming peregrinations by becoming Fenyves Jenö. He was nationalist like the others and, like his brother Aladár was to do a few years later, he "Hungarianized," "Magyarized" his name, from Finkelstein to Fenyves (or in one instance in a photograph, Fenyvesi, with an *i*). Then, once adopted, he became Fenyves-Luy (on another photograph he is Fenyves Luy, without the hyphen—you can see how the past is elusive, uncertain). Then he became Luy György and a Catholic. (Long after my grandfather's death I found, in my mother's linen closet, a lawyer's diploma on genuine parchment with an enormous red wax seal protected by an attractively carved wooden box. The diploma stated that the *Ornatissimus Dominus Georgius Luy annorum œetatis XXVII* belonged to the *Religionis Rom. Cath.* Even better: I found his baptismal certificate.) You follow me? Bravo. You must be hip; you too, must have some hidden antecedents somewhere: are they Jewish? Eastern European? Or, *horribile dictu*, both? Say, are you from Over There?

So, the two Finkelstein brothers were called Luy and

Fenyves. (And what of the other children? I know that there were many of them, but I know nothing about them, except the names on a birth certificate. No one spoke to me about them, neither my grandparents, nor my mother. Why?)

But the Great Saint, blessed be His name, is an obstinate and unfair player when dealing with those trying to challenge Him. He is a sore loser. He knows what He wants, the path for each being is drawn not from his or her birth but from the creation of the world, and it is not the will of a small Jew, though Hungarian Catholic, though Transylvanian, at times Finkelstein, at times Fenyves or Fenyvesi, at times Fenyves Luy or Luy and Jenö then György, that is going to change the original, preestablished order of things. The die was cast long ago: The Eternal, blessed be His name, had decided that this Catholic was to remain a Jew—and he did.

During a trial, György met a witness, the most charming of the young Jewish women of the area. The rest of the story would be banal except for the fact that this meeting ended up forcing our petty noble Catholic to become a Jew again. The young woman was very religious, and neither she nor her family would have tolerated her marrying a *goy*, even a Jewish one, and particularly not if he had been a Jew *to begin with*. György thus agreed to reconvert to Judaism. But this was not to be taken lightly by the local rabbi and his Holy Boss. Even though the rabbi agreed that György could keep his new name, he forced him to go through the complete conversion process that involved relearning the Hebrew he had long forgotten, the liturgy, and the rest. The result was that in the whole of the Finkelstein and Perlmutter (the name of the new spouse) family, it was the complete atheist neobeliever, a- and antireligious, who had the best knowledge of the Torah, the Talmud and the interpretation of the Parashot.

The Doctor in Jurisprudence, Luy György became a great and fat lawyer in Budapest, a man of broad culture and physical strength, a funny fun-loving bon-vivant. I loved him, he loved me. I was his sole grandchild. We would roughhouse in bed when I was made to take a nap and he liked to take one, too. One day, he threw me off the bed and I hit my head—I screamed, more for the form than from the pain, and my grandmother rushed in. She too was screaming, but from anger against "the old fool." He liked to keep his brain challenged: he read a lot, did crossword puzzles, collected and classified jokes, bons mots, stamps, and above all, he was a passionate chess player. He often played with my father (who would beat him despite my grandfather's cheating), and also by himself, copying famous games he found in a chess manual.

*Allow me to tell you one of his jokes, a bit excessive as jokes have to be if they are to draw laughter. What is worse: a Hungarian anti-Semite or a philo-Semite? The philo-Semite, of course, because he is obviously a liar to boot.*

He used to walk to work. He liked the walk. The courthouse was close by in the center of Budapest. His wife, my grandmother Blanka, Perlmutter Blanka (whom my grandfather, even though he did not know a word of French used to call Blanche), used to say that this walk was very good for him. My grandfather concurred with her opinion and he would stop at eleven o'clock in the morning always in the same café-restaurant after having eaten a substantial breakfast at home. They knew him well there: good morning sir, the usual? Yes, a veal paprika goulash with your freshly made noodles, *nokedlis*, and a cucumber salad with sour cream and garlic, and of course a small beer, a *pikolo*. This was deadly for him, my grandmother supposedly only made him nonfat dishes (I doubt this, given the time and Hungarian cooking habits . . .), and there was no alcohol on the table because my grandfather had advanced heart disease, and had already two heart attacks to his name. The family gossip is that he would meet his brother Aladár in this restaurant, almost every day, after the war, during and in spite of their wives' enmity.

He died of a heart attack at age sixty-eight, very suddenly, leaving behind him, in him, the war. The war he spent in a Budapest suburb at the home of compassionate and brave Bulgarian vegetable dealers, hidden with my grandmother under their mattress in the bedding drawer. And then in the fifties, he was the victim of a hit and run accident when an army truck ran over him in a pedestrian crossing and left him for dead. Grandfather did not die but, to his dying days, he had an eye and an ear lower on one side of his head than on the other, along with a host of other troubles, in the jaws, in his skull. So, against everyone's advice, he sued the People's Army of the Peoples' Republic. They predicted that he would be deported, put in prison, or even worse—very sound advice as the Hungarian stalinist regime was not fond of headstrong citizens. He sued anyway, and since he could not find another lawyer who was fearless, or intelligent, or suicidal enough, he had to be his own lawyer. You're going to laugh: he won! It took three years but he won. This shows that even in systems like that one, there are cracks, holes. Those systems are made by human beings. Sure they're bastards, but they're only human, so there are some people who create cracks in such a system and others who plunge head-long into them.

Before the war, this grandfather was on the left. An awkward position as he was living in a right-wing country and fed off its rotten system, but . . . One day he decided to stop paying taxes, because taxes were theft, particularly when this theft was perpetrated by a fascist state (his wife paid them secretly, by selling a carpet, a vase . . .). On May 1, International Labor Day, he used to go with my mother to join the forbidden protest in the city's wooded park. He carried his oversized trumpet whose horrible sound aggravated the workers who were protesting and drew the cops. In addition to his heart disease, and the war, and the terror of arrest and deportation, in addition to the accident with the truck, during World War I his right arm was hit by a bullet (need I say he was a right-handed?) while fighting at the Italian front, in Doberdo, as a lieutenant in the Austro-Hungarian army. His right hand became useless. His numb, frozen fingers fascinated me. I was amazed to see my grandfather tie his shoelaces or his bow tie with only one hand—his left one to boot.

At this point, so I can relax a bit, ease up on the trauma of these stories, and give you a break from this tangle of unpronounceable names and places and fuzzy dates, I will tell you two episodes of my grandfather's life in World War I, both told to me by my mother. The first is only an image: my mother, then an adorable four-year-old blond girl, was placed by her father, lieutenant in the occupation army, on the throne of the king of Serbia in Belgrade. The second is a story that deeply affected my mother: my grandfather was assigned to the post of commanding officer of a camp of Russian prisoners of war. He lived there with his family. The prisoners adored my mother and kept on giving her gifts. But my grandfather had forbidden my mother to accept any gifts (and perhaps also forbidden her to go to the camp and mix with the prisoners). One day, despite this, little Györgyi came back home with her arms loaded with cookies. Her father bent her over his knees and gave her such a spanking, the first and last he gave her for the whole of his life, with his military belt (he must have been in quite a rage!) that my mother could still feel the pain seventy years later.

*Russian soldiers' love for children was legendary. During the siege of Budapest, when they were raping any women they could grab, they would spare those accompanied by children. In March of '45, in the city that had been freed a month previously, my mother, trying to get home as fast as possible, was pushing me in a baby carriage on the great boulevard of Budapest (my father had not yet returned from forced labor in the mines). I can still see the scene clearly: the asphalt had been ripped in places by grenades, and replaced by wooden planks so that military trucks could pass. A convoy went by us, slowed down, and a soldier threw a package in my buggy as he laughed and yelled khleba, bread.*

I used to spend my summer vacation with my grandparents at Lake Balaton in a villa owned by my parents (this of course during a regime that forbade private property—once again, thanks to the cleverness and courage of my mother, we had been able to keep this house). My grandfather would remain all day long in his pajamas and wore a straw hat against the hot Hungarian sun. He did crosswords puzzles and played chess against himself and against boredom, listened to radio Free Europe in Hungarian against the regime, made sparkling water with cartridges against thirst, and cried when our famous soccer team (yes, you do remember correctly, it was that of Puskás, Kocsis, and Hidegkúti . . .) lost against West Germany in 1954.

*I was already living in the West, when my grandfather wrote me a letter listing all of his ailments, aches, illnesses and deformities: his heart, his stomach, his bladder, his left eye, his right hand, his excessive weight, and what have you (to my chagrin I lost that letter) and in which he encouraged me to be happy. (Is it possible? Happiness is a gift.) He, he had this gift. To him I owe my fondness for jokes, my love for women, and for quibbling. He also taught me not to take myself seriously . . . (But to whom do I owe despair? Who gave me that gift? Perhaps the time and the place.) The irrational, the attraction of the absurd, the silly rhymes, surrealism also came from him, and particularly, rebelliousness, or, to put it more humbly, disobedience. This disobedience, the impulse to first respond with a "no," came from him via my mother. As to my father, he remained silent or said yes, even while quietly doing the opposite.*

Luy, the attorney, wrote poems, tales for his daughters and friends. He had an original style and a sure feel for versification and the absurd. I am still wondering today if the silly little song he used to sing me had been composed by him or been extracted from a forgotten musical or operetta. At any rate, I never heard anyone else sing it. I can't resist the desire to write it down here, translated from the Hungarian:

*The day I was born*
*Taté asked me*
*My son what are we going to do with you,*
*What name would suit you?*

*Mamé said: Schmulé, Aron.*
*Taté said: no way.*
*When I heard this,*
*I jumped out of my crib,*
*And started screaming:*
*The most beautiful name is Grünstein Számi,*
*Hei diridirdiri ding-deng-dong.*

Here is the Hungarian original for connoisseurs and gourmets:

*Mikor a világra jöttem,*
*Tate megkérdezte tölem:*
*Fiam mit csináljunk véled,*
*Milyen nevet adjunk néked?*
*Máme mondta: Smüle, Áron.*
*Táti mondta: semmi áron.*
*Mikor én ezt meghallottam,*
*A bölcsömböl kiugrattam,*
*S elkezdtem én kiabálni:*
*A legszebb név a Grünstein Számi,*
*Hej diridirdiri ding-deng-dong.*

(It isn't possible to translate the humor of these rhymes: *áron* in Hungarian means in addition to the familiar name, "for a price." *Semmi áron* means "at no price."[1])

And then, unluckily or luckily, since I have time, since I

1. In both Hungarian and French "at no price" means in English "under no circumstance," or to put it more colloquially in the spirit of the original: "no way," "not a chance." The pun and rhyme, here in both Hungarian and French, presents a challenge to the translator. *Trans.*

have nothing else to do than to tell about *that* time and those people, I am also transcribing another one of his simple(?) poems. If this poem was not created by him, please let me know, prove it to me—I won't even be disappointed. I would be delighted, happy that someone else knows of the existence of this poem.

I would no longer be alone.

So here's this masterpiece (the original Hungarian title is "Wettenberger Wilibald"):

*Wilibald of Wettenberg*
*A fat Czech knight he was*
*Wilibald of Wettenberg.*
*One evening, a summer evening,*
*Spinach he was eating.*
*His valet came in and exclaimed:*
*"O! Wilibald! In Prague,*
*The assembly has elected*
*A king of the Czechs,*
*I thus salute you*
*Your Majesty*
*Wilibald of Wettenberg."*

*Upon hearing this happy news*
*The spinach flew against the wall.*
*"Gross food, how dare you sully*
*the mouth of a king*
*(a king of the Czech)!"*

*But the valet again flew into the room*
*"prevarication, corruption,*

*And so my lord Wilibald,*
*I must now salute you*
*As a dethroned king of the Czechs!"*

*Upon hearing this sad news*
*To the spinach splattered wall he turned*
*And licked the spinach all up*
*Wilibald of Wettenberg.*

When a righteous poverty befell the country, the Hungarian government allotted to the comrade grandparents a one room cooking sleeping studio in exchange for their one hundred and fifty square meters apartment (in Dohány utca, that is "Tobacco Street," I'll come back to this later), which they had already been forced to share with two other families. They did not complain. They both came from nothing, absolutely nothing. My grandfather was the descendent of a day laborer, a concierge, a cart driver; he was an attorney by sheer force of will . . . Oh, come on, no illusions allowed here! He did it by sheer force of chance, of persistence, of accident . . . as for my grandmother, she had been a destitute orphan at age six.

*This doesn't mean a thing. People so easily forget their ancestors, how they made their living. Look at the picture of the three W. taken by Helmut Newton; look at the faces of Salomon G., of Joseph K. . . . The grandfather of Daniel W., he tells this himself, was a humble Alsatian tailor, while the first G. also a tailor, but even poorer, left Russia with eight or twelve children, I can't remember the exact number . . . Just look at their faces now!*

# 3

# Perlmutter Blanka

My future grandmother Blanka was the youngest of the eleven Perlmutter children. (I say eleven because I only know of eleven. Six of them did not return from the camps. Four survived the war: Malvin, a school teacher in Budapest, Hungary; Eugene, a millionaire in San Francisco, United States of America; Ernest, a tailor in Boulogne-sur-Mer, France; and my grandmother. Then there was the eleventh, a metal craftsman. I still have some of his work: a chandelier, two photo frames and a small table, all made out of cast iron and all very beautiful. But I don't have his given name, nor the

date of his death. Did he die *before* or *during?* I wonder—did he go to Germany as an apprentice, did he come back just in time for . . . ?) There might have been other children who were born and died very young, while still in infancy. That's how it was then. So I can't know for sure, but I am thinking perhaps there were eleven of them. Their mother died so young—did she even have time to give birth to yet more children? Then the father, Perlmutter Farkas, who I believe was a lumber salesman, passed away right after her. It's Blanka who suffered least from the death of her parents. She was six years old; she didn't understand. (That's what the others must have been saying. But in fact, at age six . . . it's all there: the need for love, the habits of love, habits . . . Who can tell if when at fifty, during one of many sleepless nights, suddenly a very distant voice, sweet and almost unfamiliar . . . Or in the street, a smell, someone, a gesture . . . Or an old photograph . . . The wound is forever, solitude and melancholy will be there for life, at sixty still, even at one hundred . . .) Her brothers and sisters took care of her like brothers and sisters can. But she had to leave school at twelve, which explains her poor spelling that plagued her all her life, the amazing blanks in her cultural knowledge, and also her practical side, her aggressiveness, her vitality; and her sense of money, her thrift. Later, they would call her stingy. If you only knew how she had to calculate, she who hadn't, or barely had, gone to school, so that they all could have something to eat, to wear . . . She was so thrifty she could have been the inventor of the expression "saving bits of candles" and "pieces of string."[1]

1. In the French *économies de bouts de chandelles* and *économies de bouts de ficelle* are popular expressions referring to extreme thrift. *Trans.*

After my grandmother's death, my mother found boxes carefully ordered and labeled: "candle pieces" "string pieces" "shirt buttons" "buttons" "zippers" "elastics" "thumbtacks" "corks." My grandmother's husband, attorney Luy, used to call her "Hussars's lieutenant" on account of her energy. She was not bossy but definitely opinionated. At Szatmárnémeti, in Transylvania (during its Hungarian period), as a little girl she was keeping house all by herself. They were too poor to afford any help. She was cooking for four, five, six—who knows how many—in the parental house now bereft of parents—a vital place.

Blanka learned to work when she was six. She learned to do everything: to sew, iron, take care of the chickens. She knew all the secrets of cooking, how to prepare tomatoes, when to pickle cucumbers in vinegar, how to make and bring the *tcholent* (in Hungary it was called *sólet*) on the eve of Sabbath to the baker's oven. She was familiar with all the clever ways of cleaning, taking out spots, reviving, sticking, unsticking, patching—so as to make clothes and all things last, to save—it had to be done. She knew how to shop, pick, haggle, make herself respected, refuse, reject, order.

At the market, everyone still remembers Mrs. Luy shopping. Upon arrival, she would ask the first merchant how much plums cost. Regardless of the answer, she'd respond: "Thief." Then she went on to the next merchant, and so on till the last! It was only after questioning all the merchants that she would make up her mind. Even if it meant going back to one she had just accused of being a crook. You might ask, why should it matter so much? Why waste so much time? But what time? Wasted out of what? Out of life? But that was life; life was right there, right in front of you, underfoot, in the market. They talked of food, of money. Grandmother Luy (that was what I called her—Grandmother Bíró was my father's mother) never wasted time, never wasted anything, she knew the value of everything.

One day, I was lugging packages behind her as she was almost running (she was always running, she had to) on our way back from the market, I was explaining, or rather was telling my grandmother the mysteries of the universe, the light years. She was amazed.

"You sure know lots of stuff," she told me. "Is this true?"

"Grandma, I learned this at school!"

"Oh, that changes everything."

She had an immense respect for knowledge and for school, for studies.

The Luys lived above a printing shop. They were rocked in their sleep, and I along with them when I spent the night, by the regular and constant purring of the presses that spewed out the most-read daily paper in the capital. On Friday evenings, my grandmother lit candles, said her prayers. After all she had come from Szatmár—this means nothing to you? At present, the Szatmár Jews in Israel are the "blackest," the most obscure, the most fanatical fundamentalists—along with those from Munkács, the place of origin of my paternal great, great grandparents. How ironic!

My grandfather never participated in the ritual. On Saturday mornings, my grandmother went to the synagogue. It was built where Theodore Herzl's birthplace once stood. It was the biggest synagogue in Europe. She didn't go there because of pride but because she lived right next to it, no farther than 200 meters, at 12 Dohány *utca*. She went to the women's floor of the synagogue, in the penumbra of this immense and now empty structure. The Jews who used to go there could no longer attend the synagogue to thank their compassionate God for his goodness and his infinite blessings because they had gone up in smoke a short time before.

Blanka went to the synagogue to say what she had to say, and to ask what she had to ask in Hungarian, then she prayed the official prayers in Hebrew she did not understand but had learned by heart at Szatmár. The language was not the only thing she couldn't understand. Grandmother Luy could comprehend neither the idea nor the service. But she never sought to understand as understanding was of no import. They could keep on asking "the question" (as the doctors of the faith, all the doctors of all the faiths—and they were and are countless—have so often asked) as to whether in the eyes of the Creator of all things it is better to have knowledge without faith, or better to know nothing, to understand nothing, but to believe.

God did exist. He watched over us. And this, regardless of what happened. Auschwitz was a punishment that might appear unjust—her sisters, her brothers had been peaceful and good people who in no way deserved such a horrible and premature death—but we cannot understand the will and the pathways of the Eternal, thus . . . We had to keep on believing, saying, asking, praying.

Around age eighteen (at what age exactly—who knows?), Perlmutter Blanka moved from Szatmár to Budapest with her sister Malvin, the school teacher (I knew her well. During my preteen years, she was as a widow living with her daughter and son-in-law; they were true communist believers, obedient, obtuse, and above all cowardly bureaucrats who wanted to keep her from celebrating the Shabbat so they wouldn't risk getting into serious trouble). Blanka could do everything and nothing. She was working at home making hats for a hatmaker. The two sisters lived together. Malvin met a postal clerk and they were soon married. Blanka could no longer pay the rent by herself. She had to move to a home for young girls. And that was the time she met my grandfather (you might perhaps prefer the other version: they met during a trial in which she was a witness and he a lawyer). At any rate, what was true was that he was slender, handsome, with black pomaded hair and moustache, already making a good living, and in love with Blanka. They held each other for hours in her room. There was no question of doing anything else. And they also talked, and wrote each other poems. But György was becoming more and more enterprising. Blanka had to forbid him from visiting her in her room. One day he presented himself at Malvin's door to ask for her sister's hand. Mrs. School Teacher consulted all her brothers and sisters, all the family, *die ganze Mischpohe*. The lawyer György was invited one Sunday afternoon for a cup of hot chocolate at Malvin's house where the whole family had gathered to meet him. The atmosphere was icy; the family behaved with more haughtiness than the Rothschilds would have in their Vienna palace if presented with a miserable Galician suitor who was also a starving Talmudic student wearing a torn and dirty coat and sporting long dandruffy curls. György thus felt provoked to add to his reception by making outlandish anticlerical statements and professing to be an anarchist. The verdict, predictably, was cut and dry: "he is not a suitable party for you, what with his ideas, with his hidalgo, pimp-like looks . . . He looks like anything but an honest Jew—and he's not even a Jew. He's neither Jewish, nor honest. At any rate he would need to reconvert, which he would obviously refuse. He'll cheat on you, abandon you. He only wants to take advantage of you. You have no trade, no money, no wealth, no dowry, no education, no relations. You have nothing and are nothing." Blanka understood in a flash that all of this was true, and that it must mean that this young man truly loved her. She knew, better than her whole family did, that a man, so handsome, with a profession, a salary and a future, wouldn't risk entering a marriage just to sleep with somebody. She thus married Mr. Luy György, alias Finkelstein Jenö (etc.), to her family's chagrin; their objections remained even though the future husband agreed to reconvert to Judaism.

After a stilted ceremony and a sad reception peopled by glowering faces and half guessed at half innuendos, grandmother Blanka and grandfather Gyuri (the diminutive of György) lived together in perfect harmony for almost sixty years—at least as much as this is possible. The circumstances of the century did not harm their relationship, on the contrary. Wars, revolutions, persecutions brought them closer. Blanka's family, confronted with the evidence, soon accepted their marriage—but the young couple remembered the past and was not keen, particularly during the first years of their marriage, to socialize with people who had accused the husband of having dubious intentions, and reduced the bride to nothing but her female body. But as time passed, the feeling for family, the famous family ties of primitive societies, did prevail.

Blanka's ingenuity, perseverance, energy and intelligence got the Luys (they had two daughters, my mother Györgyi and Anni) out of any and all desperate situations, while my grandfather's social ease, sense of humor, impressive appearance, along with his vast knowledge all helped quickly establish his professional reputation and insured them a comfortable life, that is until World War II, and after that Stalinism, unsettled everything ... But isn't this already collective history? Yes and no, for how can we tell where lies the boundary between the individual and the group?

Grandmother Luy worshiped life. Everything alive was sacred: plants, animals—even humans—can you imagine! She was reluctant to squash a mosquito on her arm, and in summer would rather chase wasps away than kill them in a jam jar. The apartment was a garden, the balcony a forest. When my mother was still a little girl, she was given all sorts of animals: cats, dogs, turtles, potbellied pigs. I personally used to feed a canary that ended up stuffed and posed on a wrought iron branch after falling victim to the crushing weight of a guest's behind during one of the many parties my grandparents used to give. But as my mother was growing up, Blanka opposed new pets under the pretext that they were not adapted to life in a big city apartment, but it was really because she had gradually realized that she could not rely on her daughters to take proper care of them.

I'm quite familiar with that routine: "Mom, please buy us a goldfish ... I swear we'll take care of it." But then, who ends up feeding the goldfish? Who cleans the aquarium? Mom.

In truth, Blanka, was not so much afraid of the care needed by the pets than by the animals' sicknesses and the deaths. At Szatmár, there were lots of animals around the house. They were the source of much pain for Blanka because they would die when their time had come—or sooner, or later. It was in the order of things, but that order was too painful. She refused to cut off the tongue of starlings to make them talk, as well as to have cats neutered (she didn't mention this last issue to her children because it was useless and they weren't old enough—though that didn't really matter for they were never old enough). She knew that for cats to remain clean and to be able to stand being locked up in the apartment, they had to be made to lose any and all desire to fornicate and to reproduce. But my grandmother felt this aggression to be cruel and intolerable.

On the floor above us there lived a superb rust colored cat, a magnificent beast, huge, kinglike. One would have taken it for a small tiger rather than for a large cat. I must have been around ten and I admired him when I visited Dohány *utca*. It was a rare specimen of beauty and power—but still of feline grace. He sought the warmth of human bodies, of laps, where, in spite of being a sovereign male, he knew how to cuddle better than a woman . . . and received plenty of caresses. He would wander on the balcony that extended the length of the apartment and came in and out through a pet door. From his position on the third floor, the cat would observe the street and the people. He would startle with every noise made by the trucks of the printing press. He would assume a frozen, stalking, ready to pounce pose as he watched pigeons, sparrows, crows, eagles, ostriches, great white owls . . .

One Saturday evening, my grandparents had been invited for dinner. I had no school the next day and was allowed to stay the night with them. They came back on foot around midnight, the night was mild but the Budapest spring was deadly. Next to the entrance door of the building the neighbors' big rust tomcat was lying on the ground, stretched out full length, its paws bent and rigid. There was no possibility of misidentification, of error; there was no other cat like him. There was no blood, just a cadaveric immobility, the preferred stance of the inhabitants of the Other World. (Grandmother Luy was sure that all animals went to heaven, in contrast to human beings, since animals were all good, even the wild ones, even the predators; they were good instinctively, automatically because of their innocence.) The grandparents were both startled and frightened. In spite of the late hour, and even before going back to their own apartment, Blanka rang the neighbors' doorbell. They knew them well, entertained each other often. She had to ring several times, the neighbors had just fallen soundly asleep, that first sleep that is said to be the deepest, the sleep of the dead. Finally, my grandparents heard "what is it" as the door opened.

"It's us, Luy Blanka and Gyuri, we are sorry to wake you up."

A hairy man appeared in his badly buttoned pajamas, a bit ridiculous looking, and scratching his scalp.

"Something awful happened: your cat fell off the balcony. We haven't touched him . . ."

As she spoke, Blanka suddenly became ashamed. They should have acted instead of unloading on the neighbors as they were doing. Even though it wasn't their cat. One must be involved . . . but she had been too upset; they had run up to the neighbors without thinking. They worried about the neighbor's reaction because he was very attached to his pet. But they couldn't be tactful under the circumstances, and at that time of they night, they were too upset to even think of tact.

"I know, I know" said the neighbor. "The idiot didn't pay

attention. He tried to catch a bird. And they say cats are agile! But thanks anyway and good night."

My grandparents were flabbergasted. Could their neighbor be drunk? But not only did he understand perfectly well what they were telling him, but worse, he already *knew it!* They looked at each other, "do you think we should do something? Of course not, he's going to get dressed and go downstairs. But why didn't he do it right away?"

They had trouble falling asleep. Where would the cat be buried? There was no public park in the neighborhood. What to do?

The next morning was a Sunday and we slept late, all three of us. Around eleven o'clock we went out together to go to the museum. My grandparents had decided not to tell me about the cat. "One of these day, soon enough, he'll notice he's no longer there. And that'll be soon enough." They would then give the grandson a vague explanation. The incident would be erased and then forgotten. The boy had to be protected. The key word was "shush." Shush, all is well. There was no talk of sex, money, politics—particularly not politics—nor of violence, death, illness, accidents, crime, war, in short, no talk of life's problems. All was well (a few years previously, life, all of it and as naked as the truth, had clenched its fist around my elders and the others, the whole country and the whole of Europe. And all the shushed protected children, bloody and broken, were held in its grip. So by then, even if stalin and his buddies played their game of terror, it was peace. And thenceforth we the children had to be spared any visible horror).

We were thus on our way to the museum since grandfather had promised me.

In front of the door, in the street, the dead cat still lay on the ground. Passersby stopped, then stepped over or walked around him.

I didn't even have the time to open my mouth in surprise or of . . . ? Grandma was already at the neighbor's who was still asleep . . . Five minutes later, wearing a blue-striped robe, he was down in the street wrapping the cat's body in newspaper.

Blanka stopped talking to him and pointedly ignored his greetings.

In September of 1952, when my grandparents came back from Lake Balaton where we had spent the summer, the concierge told them that in July the neighbor and his wife, who had been the owners of a factory before the war, had been arrested and taken away, like so many others. No one had heard from them since. Blanka said nothing. Not a word. The next Saturday, at the synagogue, she tearfully begged for forgiveness from the Eternal because she had felt no sorrow when hearing the news, and perhaps even . . .

# 4

## Bíró Mariska

My paternal grandmother was called Hirschl Mariska (or Mária—her given names kept changing on the various certificates and identity pieces I found) before she became Bíró Márkné, that is Mrs. Bíró Márk. It seems strange to me for a Jew to have that name, even though the name of the biblical Mary was Miriam. It was not customary to use this name, and still isn't, as far as I know. But that's the way it goes. Whence this troubling thing: one of Mária's sons, my uncle, was named József, Joseph. From husband of the biblical Mary, he became son. Can you guess my grandmother

Biró Ádám ükapja

Hegedűs Péter II

passionately loved this son whom she preferred over my father. So we can well understand her extreme grief upon her beloved child's untimely death.

Grandmother Bíró enjoyed many gifts: she was constantly writing with an angular and unique handwriting. As a young girl, she wrote poems, then as a widow, a novel and a long text on the martyrdom of her loved ones, then, toward the end of her life, radio plays. She was superb at crochet (I managed to save quite a few pieces of her work) and she could draw very well. She had had the luck of being able to cultivate her talents: she came from a rather well off family. Her father owned a flourishing shoe store in Nagyvárad, in Transylvania . . .

*But . . . all of a sudden there is a stroke of lightening, a flash of memory: didn't he go bankrupt? And the flash becomes light; yes, hurray! I remember now: my shoe salesman great grandfather Hirschl Berndt went bankrupt! And this brings yet another story to mind, as it was told by Géza, my father's cousin. It's the story of one of my grandmother's wealthy relatives. I don't know what he was doing, what was his profession, his name, our degree of kinship—on what step of the ladder he is located, from what branch of the genealogical tree he is hanging? He might have been either a brother or cousin of Hirschl Berndt, but what I do know, he was a wealthy playboy. I was told that every Saturday he would be wandering the streets of the town, always the same town, Nagyvárad, with three horse drawn buggies. In the first was the* cigánybanda, *that is the tzigane band, he was in the second, and in the third were his gloves, top hat, and cane. Si non è vero, è ben trovato. Finally, I'm proud. I'm proud of having as ancestors a poor peasant, a wealthy man about town, and a bankrupt merchant. In short I'm proud of having—of having had—a family like all other families.*

*A gettó, után*

From the outset, grandmother Bíró was never friend with grandmother Luy because of the difference of class, so-cial origin and wealth. This sort of thing is not easily forgot-ten, even though grandparents Luy became much better off than grandparents Bíró. Grandmother Bíró was educated, cultured; grandmother Luy was uneducated. And while this latter was resourceful, thrifty and an excellent cook, the first had been brought up like a princess in her parents' house (one of three daughters and six sons), she was adored and spoiled by the husband, had two sons and a maid at her disposal or under her commands. She didn't know how to do anything practical, in spite of her artistic gifts. She couldn't do anything manual in spite of the agility of her ten fingers. She was a lady by birth and an artist by behavior. The other grandmother was born and remained a worker, in spite of the money her husband was bringing in.

Mariska remained a lady till World War II. In 1944 my grandparents were locked up in the Nagyvárad ghetto from which their son Józsi (the diminutive of József) got them out. As soon as they were freed, they came up to Budapest and stayed with us, that is with their son Imre, my father, in the hope of spending the war there in safety.

Fate had decided otherwise.

My grandmother's life was destroyed on the day a neighbor came to tell us that her husband and her beloved son were dead. She was broken, destroyed, crushed, annihilated, erased in a way beyond anything you could possibly imagine.

In 1945, as soon as the war ended, Mariska went back to her home, her apartment in Nagyvárad, to live with her memories and the traces of presences. But in 1952 she definitely left her native Transylvania, which has since become Romanian, and her town, which has since become Oradea. She returned to Budapest, which had since become communist, to join the rest of her family, or at least what was left of it: my father, my mother, me, as well as her only brother Nándor, with whom she settled (all of her other brothers and sisters alive in 1944 had been exterminated). She had not been able to stand the empty house, the memories, the traces, the absences. She wasn't able to stand herself. On a 1938 photograph, I can see an elegant young woman, ramrod straight, just as my father stood. On another, she is there with her husband and a small child, me. She seems to have already aged twenty years; on that photo my grandmother had written: "after the ghetto." Finally, a photograph shows her on my father's arm in 1947: an elderly woman, dressed in black, bent, shoulders sagging, cheeks hollow . . . This photo was taken in Nagyvárad, and I was also in it.

*It's the only time I visited this mythical town, the cradle of one side of my family. I was six years old, I went there with my father. I remember the endless journey; I vomited twice. I also remember our arrival. At the station we took a buggy to go to my grandmother. We must have been there for quite a while because I retain several memories of my stay: I am "working" in the shoemaker's shop in my grandmother's street, Strada Bariciu in Indo-European (Iványi Ödön utca in Finno-Ugric). I am gluing and hammering on a small bench. For my hard work, the shoemaker gives me a pair of red ankle boots he custom-made for me. One morning we are in the process of eating breakfast when my grandmother gives me some pennies to put in the drum of a bear that a peasant is making dance under our window. I go to it and, encouraged by the bear-tamer, I caress the rough fur of the enormous beast that is twice my height and hovers over me. Then, there are Russian soldiers who come to search my grandmother's apartment. They find nothing suspicious. I am not afraid. I know them from Budapest. Two years previously a soldier who had been wounded in front of our house had been brought to our underground shelter by his fellow soldiers. My mother (or someone else) wanted to give him a shot—the Soviet soldier who had never seen a syringe trampled it.*

My mother did not like her mother-in-law. She often told me so, but only after my grandmother had died. Before, she hadn't uttered a word of this to me. She accused her of being selfish, then as my mother was getting older, she blamed her for my father's faults which seemed to her increasingly numerous as time went by. My father was a very good son, obedient; he addressed his parents formally all his life and fulfilled all of a son's—a good son's—duties. As he was dying, he specifically asked to be buried next to his mother—which hurt my feelings, but I respected his wishes. My mother, whom I had cremated, rests, also at her request, next to her parents and her sister—death has thus frozen forever their mutual lack of understanding of body and spirit.

From that day in January of 1945 when my grandmother heard the news of the killing of her loved ones, till her own death in 1970, she cried every single night. And I mean, every single night, without exception. She sometimes spent the night at our house and I can still hear her laments, her cries. She had one sole topic of conversation: this tragedy. Everything led her back to it. If we talked about cooking, she'd mention their favorite dishes; about fashion, their clothes; about Nagyvárad, she broke down in sobs . . .

She had died with them.

Her old age was pitiful. Nándor and she, two shriveled old folk, looking like sick and plucked birds, lived in a dark apartment whose windows opened onto one of the many noisy and gloomy internal courtyards of an enormous turn of the century building of metal and with the circular hallways typical of the cities of the Austro-Hungarian empire—Budapest, Vienna, Prague. She would crochet, order her brother about, harass their third roommate, an old mousy friend from Nagyvárad, and obey and idolize an energetic, hypocritical, and very dishonest housekeeper. Because my grandfather Bíró had been deprived of the right to a retirement pension, my parents gave her what she needed to live; she had no other resource, no wealth.

# 5

## Bíró Márk

My father's father, Bíró Márk, was born in Hungary in 1879.

*Everyone in this family of aliens had been born in Hungary. It's enough to cause despair in the ranks of the Hungarian Life and Truth Party, the ridiculous extreme right wing ultranationalists.*

He was born in Királyhelmec, in Zemplén County. His father was a teacher in Tiszaföldvár, a village on the Tisza, in the very heart of peasant, earth-bound Hungary, in the heart of the great plain, the *puszta*. I wouldn't able to point out

Tiszaföldvár on a map, but strangely, I am not interested in it, or barely so. As to Királyhelmec, I've never heard anyone talk about it. My father never once uttered the name of his father's native village—unlike me, as my daughters would attest.

He was born Braun Márkus, but when still very young he modernized his given name by deleting its Latin ending, then "Hungarianized" his family name into Bíró, a word that can be translated into English as "judge" or "arbiter," or "mayor of a small county."

*The verb bírni means "to be able," but also "to possess," "to hold." The etymology of bíró is also "the one who can possess." Unfortunately, Bíró is a very common Hungarian name. I say unfortunately because all of the Bírós or Biros of Paris have already phoned me to ask if we are related (we've never found a kinship link, I am the relative of no other Bíró), or to suggest that I publish their amateurish water colors. There are several famous Bírós, of whom one, Lajos, also from Nagyvárad, was a very talented writer who lived before and after World War I; another, Miklós, was a communist graphic artist who escaped from Russia after the defeat of the Republic of the Soviets in 1919, and cre-*

ated a great number of remarkable protest and revolutionary posters. The most famous, László, who went by Ladislas, was a Hungarian who lived in France and died in Argentina, and invented the ball point pen. It is because of him that they used to say in English: "Do you have a biro?" or in Italian "una biro" and in Argentina, of course they said "una birome." One day, as we were arriving late in the evening on the main plaza in Killarney, what do we see written in neon letters in the Irish sky, above an enormous merry-go-round? Biro! But none of these Biros, some of them Jewish and some of them not, were part of our family.

Braun Márkus Hungarianized his name at the moment when the patriotism of Hungarian Jews was at its peak (some good it did them—just as it did Captain Dreyfus, the most French of the French, the most stupid of patriots).

*Franz-Joseph had been emperor of Austria since 1848 and king (crowned even! Along with Sissi herself!) of Hungary since 1867. During his reign, Hungarian Jews were emancipated and able to fully participate in the life of the nation. At least that's what they hoped. They got rid of their German or Jewish names or both. Finkelstein became Fenyves or Fenyvesi or Fenyö, Lœwinger became Lakatos, Kohn became Kardos or Kertész, Singer Somogyi, Rosenberg Rózsa, the National Nemzeti, the Liberty Libamáj (these last two can only make Hungarians laugh, though it has to be on a good day—nemzeti means "national," and labamáj means "foie gras"). And the Braun became Bokor or Bodor . . . or Bíró (it was said that the new names kept the same first letters so that monograms on shirts and handkerchiefs wouldn't need to be changed . . . ). They also gave up their language: no one spoke Yiddish in my family. (I write this for form's sake: Hungarian Jews, those from the heart of the country, never did speak Yiddish. Russian, Polish, and*

*Lithuanian Jews spoke it. In the Austro-Hungarian Empire, Yiddish was only still spoken on border areas, in Galicia, Ruthenia, Bucovina … ) And then, the urban population also got rid of its faith. It produced politicians, journalists, writers, photographers, filmmakers, and world famous musicians. Most of the lawyers, doctors, bankers in Budapest were Jewish. But they all, down to the last individual, thought of themselves as Hungarian and openly claimed that identity. And yet, they were Jewish and Hungarian, they couldn't be one without the other (one day my father told me, "Jews are very intelligent, Hungarians very creative, so, a Hungarian Jew is the apex of the human species." I believed him for a long time. And, all shame set aside, I must confess that I might still believe it, perhaps secretly or at least unconsciously).*

My grandfather Márk's love for Hungary was extreme. When Transylvania became Romanian between the two world wars, he was the president of the Hungarian party. (Just as my great-uncle Nándor was the deputy of the Hungarian minority in the Romanian parliament in Bucharest.) Then he decided to ignore the prohibition of teaching Hungarian history in high school. The Romanian government fired him for this nationalistic action. In my father's papers, I found the thick file with the letters and the petitions and appeals in which Márk was trying to become reinstated in the Hungarian pension system after the Hungarian retook Transylvania.

*A bit of laughter in the midst of this sad story: Transylvania was Hungarian, became Romanian in 1919, then Hungarian again in 1938 and then Romanian in 1945. . . . Did you notice that in these stories all the names always keep on changing but nothing really changes? Finkelstein into Luy, Jenö into György, Braun into Bíró, but that's not all: Bíró into Biro, Ádám into Adam, the Hungarian Erdély into the Roma-*

*nian Ardeal, and then back into Erdély, then into Transylvania—but
the core itself remained immutable.*

My patriotic and nationalist grandfather's letters were addressed to heads of department, to the minister of education, and to the governor, horthy-the-puke himself.

*When I think that this minuscule piece of vomit excreted by the earth
is now resting in, under Hungarian soil; when I think that there has
been a Hungarian government cowardly or stupid (or bastardly?)
enough to bring back this scum's remains from Portugal and to bury
them with pomp and ceremony—even giving school children a day
off! But the present government (I'm writing this in 2002) also put up
a plaque in honor of the Hungarian gendarmerie. And to think that it
was the Hungarian police that committed the deportation of the Jews
during the war—often against German orders—yes, I know of some
specific examples, "Yes, he says, and who do you think sought out the
Paris Jews to drag them to the Vél d'Hiv?[1] Do you prefer French cops to
Hungarian cops?" "But God, who was it that created cops? And who
created human beings in such a way that they need cops?"*

The letters date from 1944. In January 1945, he was murdered on the ground that he was a Jew, that he was a foreigner. His murderers came into power thanks to the people to whom his petitions were addressed.

I barely knew him. I was three when he died. I have many

1. *Vél d'Hiv* is the usual abbreviation in both English and French for a sports
stadium called the Winter Velodrome. It refers to the roundup in July 1942 of
12,884 Parisian Jews who were sought out and arrested by the French police
under the initiative of French officials and kept there for five days under horrendous conditions before being sent to concentration camps. *Trans.*

photos and caricatures of him because he was a public person—the principal of the Jewish high school of a very Jewish city, even the commander of the civil guard in 1918, between the end of the war and the Romanian occupation. He was a dyed-in-the wool franc-mason (convinced of what? Of the Great Architect's wisdom?), a Hungarian patriot—was he a believer? A religious, practicing Jew? Could his beliefs allow him this? Could he, the principal of a Jewish high school dependent on the Jewish community's donations not be a religious, practicing Jew? I know through newspaper articles and the letters that I found, and also through a magnificent album with fine leather covers, made specifically for him as a present for his twenty-five years of service to the school, that he was respected, loved, honored by everyone. He was somebody. On the photographs he is always elegantly dressed; very handsome, with noble features of an Oriental Semitic type. He had the Sephardi looks with his olive skin, his very black hair, moustache and eyes as dark as my father's, as my grandfather Luy's, as dark as mine. (In May 2001, in my parents' almost completely empty apartment I found, under the last piece of furniture that was to be taken away, a photo showing my grandfather when he was twenty years old: "Photo Rivoli, Budapest." I again was struck by his appearance, his Oriental features. There was nothing Ashkenazi about him. Our ancestors must have been kicked out of Spain in 1492, taken refuge with the sultan, and then come to Transylvania along with the Turks in the sixteenth century. The Turks left, but the Jews stayed. This calls for the sort of research that I won't do.)

I remember only one image of him. The year is 1944. I have come down with whooping cough and he is carrying me on his shoulders in the street leading to the city's gas plant so that I can breathe in the gas fumes because it was thought that this would cure a cough (thirty-seven years later when my asthma was diagnosed, the doctor said, "Tell me, do you cough when you laugh?"). I ask my grandfather to buy me a roll, a *buci*. I am wearing my tiny coat made of lamb skin with the fur in the inside and decorated on the outside with Hungarian style appliqués. I am three years old. I don't know anything, I am alive, I ask for a *buci*.

He handed down to my father, and from my father to me, the sense of duty, of honesty, of work, of virtue, and of other nonsense. And also the fear of what people would say, the need to maintain appearances. Till the last of his days, my father always behaved as if his father, as father and school principal, could see him. The principal had been severe. You could read it in his eyes (even though he did carry me on his back). He must have been the opposite of bon vivant grandfather Luy, the funny man, always in search of a clever repartee, the cheater, dressed in his pajamas.

The arrow-cross, the Hungarian nazi effectively came into power in October of 1944, and from that time on, there was no longer any "protected house" (protected by the Red Cross, the knights of Malta, Sweden, Switzerland, Outer Mongolia, Botswana, the Salomon Islands—all wanted to save us, one wonders why they didn't), no longer any refuge safe for the Budapest Jews (the Jews from the provinces had already been deported). It was deadly dangerous for them to be seen in the street. My uncle Józsi absolutely wanted to go get his things he had left in a basement or an apartment in—I even remember the name of the street—Nap *utca*, Sun Street. His "things": winter coats, sweaters . . . Since he was deaf, my mother had to go along, just in case . . . But my mother was not ready; she was in the process of feeding me. Józsi was impatient; by nature as impatient as my father and me. He did not want to, could not wait for my mother, and so my grandfather decided to go with his son.

They never came back.

Young arrow-cross hoodlums stopped them on Oktogon Plaza. A newspaper seller who knew them from Nagyvárad yelled out: "These two, they're Jews, I know them." They were brought into a building belonging to the arrow-cross members. They were only after my uncle (why?) and were willing to let my grandfather go. He refused to leave his deaf son alone. They were tortured (with a razor blade, I know this though I have never dared tell this to anyone because I didn't want to think about it, I didn't dare imagine the scene, even my parents did not know about it. It was Auer Anikó who told me. My grandfather wiped off the blood on his son's back with his shirt), then they were led near the Lánchíd, the hanging bridge. There, on the shore of the Danube, they were tied together and one of them was shot so that the dead one would pull the living one to the bottom of the water. Did the father drag the son in? Or was it the other way around?

How can one still believe in the One who allowed this, who ordered this to happen?

I lived for another twelve years in that country. In that city, not too far from that bridge, where my parents lived more than fifty years. We shook hands, greeted people in the bus, looked peoples in the eyes; I politely let my elders ahead of me through the bakery's door as I had been taught. Fifty-four years later, I am typing this on my iBook, I feel miserable, tears run down silently on my cheek.[2] I sniffle.

Per chance a neighbor from our street was arrested in the same raid. But he was able to free himself from his bounds and, I don't know how, get out of the icy water, and he came to tell us all this two weeks later.

*This story fed me, made me. Among the many things I owe to this period (my refusals, my hatreds, my fears) and what I owe to this narrative in particular, is this trait: my aversion for things, for* holmik, *and their ownership. I have an old obsession for hotel rooms, or for empty rooms . . . I collect nothing and can't understand the collector's mentality.*

One of Józsi's mistresses was the daughter of an arrow-cross official. It was my mother who told it to me (could this really be true?). She told me that if my grandfather had returned home, the family could have tried to let that woman know what was happening, and she might have been able to intervene. Why did my mother tell me this? All her life she had implicitly and explicitly accused her husband's family, the Bíró family, of every weakness, every fault. (In fact, as I wrote earlier, this aversion was essentially aimed at grandmother Bíró.) Was this yet another way of accusing them? Or, more likely, it could have been to her deeply desperate and pessimistic nature one further proof of the absurdity of life? At the end of Camus's *Misunderstanding*, Maria asks the servant who had been silent during the whole play: "Please take pity of me, help me!" and he answers, "No!"

This murder happened on January 6, 1945. Budapest was

---

2. And a couple of years later on the translator's cheek. *Trans.*

to be liberated by the Soviet army on February 13, and the whole of Hungary on April 4. France had been freed for a long time already. Each year on the sixth of January, my parents threw two red roses into the Danube, and grandmother Bíró till the last of her days refused to cross the river. When she was forced to take one of the bridges to go from Pest to Buda, for instance when she went to my father's hospital, she would close her eyes so as not to see that water, that river.

# 6

## Uncles Eugene and Ernest

I'm in Paris, among my cousins yet all alone, far away, facing the big box filled with photographs, old family photos—from France, Hungary, and elsewhere. These photographs are like those owned by all, or almost all, families, at least by those History allowed to preserve their histories. I am aware of the reason why I'm feeling a sudden nostalgia when looking at this old picture of a man I haven't known and whose features can barely be made out. It is because for me, this man at the wheel of his car brings me back to my Hungarian childhood, yes that very man on this very photograph from

America, 1915. But then, as the opening words of one of my favorite films say, "the past is a foreign country. Things are different there . . ."[1]

The picture is on a postcard sent from San Francisco in July (the specific day is unreadable) 1915, 8:30 p.m. and it arrived in Boulogne-sur-Mer, "Boulogne ˢ/Mer —Pas ᵈᵉ Calais" at 12:45. Lower down, in the middle of the round stamp, one can make out: 25-, the rest is fuzzy. The two cents vermilion postage stamp representing the Panama Canal has been cancelled with a long stamp: WORLD'S PANAMA-PACIFIC EXPOSITION 1915.

Uncle Eugene, the sender and subject of the photo postcard, is holding a huge cigar between his lips; he wears a strange round hat, rigid and low, pulled down over his eyes and held up by his ears, of which only the left one visible. Both his hands hold the wheel of a car with the license plate 81845. The car is small, its roof is down. It was surely a very recent model at the time (could it be the legendary Model T?). But today its bygone appearance elicits a smile. In fact it looks more like a buggy than a car and is reminiscent of a comic film. The car's wheels are enormous, as is the windshield made of two parts that look like they can be folded down in good weather. Uncle Eugene, sitting high in his car as if it were the top of a hill, is proudly grasping the enormous steering wheel and staring at the camera. The contraption occupies the whole of the photo, and Uncle Eugene seems small in the midst of this mechanical mass: rods, plaques, rivets, bolts, pipes, cables, crowbars, plugs, handles . . . And yet, he is the one dominating the scene, and

1. The film is *The Go-Between* (1970), directed by Joseph Losey. *Trans.*

even today, when the spectator-onlooker's mechanical curiosity should be aroused by this vehicle from another age, it is Uncle Eugene whom the voyeur-mechanic first notices.

Eugene Perlmutter arrived in San Francisco from his native Transylvania in 1905. Eugene was also called Jenö, just like my grandfather Finkelstein Jenö, his future brother-in-law, the attorney Luy György. He was a glazier apprentice. The year 1905 was the year of the great San Francisco earthquake: the glass maker, who was smart, capable, and had the feel for business, made his fortune. I never knew the truth. Was Eugene really a glazier? And what did they mean by "made his fortune" at Szatmárnémeti, on the eve of World War I? Did the word "fortune" have the same meaning in California, on the Pacific shore, as it did on the sandy shore of the Körös, in the great Hungarian plain where poor peasants fed (or tried to feed) a whole family on a single acre of wheat? But visibly Eugene fed the legend of which he was perhaps the creator: the car, the cigar, the pose . . . the uncle from America. The photo was all the more posed in that the car is obviously neither moving, nor just stopped as the wheels, slightly dug into the sand, give the impression that the car was displayed a few centimeters away form the paved road. Besides, the uncle isn't driving it; he is happy just to hang on to the wheel, his two hands clenched, or rather we could say firmly holding it, clearly an owner's hands. And his gaze, straight into the eye of the camera, is saying: "Do you see me? It's me, it's mine."

*"Just look at those owners' hands!" On Ingres's painting of* Monsieur Bertin, *in the Louvre: "his fingers are hooks, it's me they are grasping! They are talons, vulture's claws."*

*"Yes, but when I say 'it's me'" I am saying 'me,' and if I did not say 'me' I would no longer exists . . ."*

*"Oh yeah . . . How about 'we' . . ."*

*"So you want to melt into the great whole? Disappear? But one must live. To be. And to be, we have to inscribe ourselves into the world. Seek honors, titles . . ."*

*"Medals, diplomas, ribbons, membership cards, credit cards, a feather in your ass . . ."*

*"The acknowledgment of others, of those around you."*

In Europe, in Transylvania, in Boulogne-sur-Mer, elsewhere as well, there was war. Already for a whole year. A useless carnage. But the mail was still working. The postcard is addressed to

> Mons, P, Ernest,
> 26 Rue Thiers,
> Boulogne ˢ/m
> France

The address with all those commas has thus been typed on a typewriter, this is all the more strange because the text itself is handwritten, sideways on the back of the card, and in Hungarian:

> I kiss you, your kid brother,
> *Jenö*

There are three mistakes in the text that, in Hungarian, only take two words: "kiss you"—one word, "your kid brother"—one word. The accents (there should have been three of them) are missing. Either Eugene had forgotten Hungarian in ten years, or more likely, he had never learned to write it correctly, except for his name. Did a secretary type the address? In any case, the contrast between the two sides of the card is striking, and if the uncle wanted a reaction, he certainly succeeded: a long address, ten black words typed on a machine—administrative, imposing—and on the other side, three blue handwritten words sentimentally, coquettishly, aesthetically across the page . . . In fact, the whole of the card conveys only one thing: "Look bro, I succeeded." Eugene has nothing to tell his older brother in his far away country where he was probably already drafted. He asks no question, but his message is loud and clear, and that is the only aim of the two sides of the postcard.

The recipient of this message was Uncle Ernö, his name Frenchified into Ernest and of whom they never spoke at home when I was a child, in contrast to Uncle Eugene who was a frequent topic of conversation. Eugene was still living in America when I was a little boy in Hungary, while Ernest had already died for France in 1916, and forever.

Ernest Perlmutter was a tailor. Perhaps he too had left for America with his brother Eugene? We will never know. Those who might have known have taken what they knew with them to the All Knowing one . . . Did Ernest remain in France for the sake Aunt Lucie's eyes, which we assume must have been beautiful? Was there not enough money to get on the ship? No one knows. Uncle Ernest is now no more than the name of a Hungarian Jew with Germanic resonance on a French memorial monument dedicated to French dead while aunt Lucie exists only as the memory of a few survivors and as an entry on the account book of a Genevan jeweler who sold her a little Rolex watch set with diamonds and who was fixing it for free, as is done in Geneva for good customers. Perlmutter Ernö thus left, like his brother Jenö in 1905 for the west, for the wide world, to flee poverty, anti-Semitism, obscurity, obscurantism, hopelessness, toward the hope of hope. He stopped somewhere on the shore of the sea— which must have been the first time he saw it. I move my head up and down while writing this—of course, who had seen the sea in Transylvania in 1905? I laugh, I have to laugh, the idea is so absurd. This Ernest who had never seen the sea ended up dying by the sea, in this far corner of Europe, the Dardanelles. This place, in spite of the musical quality of its name, was only known prior to the Club Med era for its murderous role without which no one would have even heard of it. Ernö stopped by the sea in Boulogne, at Wimereux, and around there he met Lucie Grunbaum—I don't know what happened, I wasn't in France then, that's for sure, I'm laughing, I wasn't even born yet, what's the use of all this, of all these family legends? Ernö fell in love with Lucie, he didn't even know French, not one word, you can be quite sure that a Transylvanian tailor could only speak Hungarian.

How was Ernö able to marry, and even, prior to that, how was he able to court a woman without speaking her language? That was because they did not talk to each other; it wasn't necessary at that time, unlike today when spouses "communicate." At that time they had to survive more than they had to communicate; they each had their assigned tasks— the man outside, the woman inside. They would meet now and then, often, on the threshold to make children, without speaking to each other. Ernest was an excellent tailor, times were hard, perhaps Lucie was very poor, or even an orphan, she needed someone to support her, a man, and since on top of this Ernö was quite handsome . . . Perhaps Ernö learned French very fast, at any rate fast enough to whisper sweet nothings into Lucie's ear . . . Or was it a community match-maker, a French *shadchen* (did they exist?) who took care of him, weighing the potential spouses' respective advantages against this temporary linguistic inconvenience? Regard-less, they got married. Ernö changed his name into Ernest, more exotic, less Hungarian, and they had three children. Ernest was handicapped by his name of Perlmutter, which, for his clientele of chic ladies from Boulogne, Roubaix, and even Lille, did not sound exotic but rather Krautish. In his la-dies tailor's shop Perlmutter Ernö thus transformed himself into "Ernest P" without a period, an appellation that might have been mysterious, romantic, strange, who knows, but it must have worked, since even the mailman who brought him the postcard from his San Francisco brother knew him by that name.

But who is to say that Uncle Ernest did receive this post-card? Where was he in 1915? Perhaps at the front line, surely already at the front? Not yet in the Dardanelles where death was already growing impatient, but elsewhere—it's his wife who got the card she couldn't read since it was written in Hungarian, or maybe the children, the oldest one yelled "Mom! Mom! A card from America! For Papa!" And Lucie, who knew Eugene (personally?—did she meet him before he embarked? Or through a photograph?) wiped off a tear, "put it there with your daddy's things, it's from his brother, oh, look at that nice car, he'll read it when he comes home on leave." Did he see it, the card with the car and the cigar, and the Hungarian mistakes? Did he reply? He had enlisted

71

to fight against his native country so as to deserve his brand new (or promised?) naturalization, so as to live *glücklich wie Gott in Frankreich*,[2] happy as a clam in France, so he went to die in a distant sea, far, very far away from Szatmár, and this for a foreign country—or not that foreign since his three children were born there . . . but a country where it was not advisable to call himself by his name, and a simple P (no period) was better than a real name, Perlmutter.

As for Eugene—and here it is the legend that speaks— glazier by profession, he arrived in San Francisco at the time of the great earthquake. That is what they told to us. I heard it a hundred, a thousand times. During the whole of my childhood. It sounded good, too good, but after all, there are people, every week, who win the lottery, there has to be, so why could he not be a glazier in San Francisco in 1905? Is it really necessary to have tears flow in the *shtetls*, ghettos, and other such resorts where Jews are all and always and everywhere massacred? (It is not necessary, but that the way it is. *Note from the Editorial Department.*) Uncle Eugene became a millionaire in San Francisco because he had the right profession at the right time and in the right place, and because precisely at that moment, in that place, Jews were not being massacred. That's it. He too, was ashamed to be called Perlmutter Jenö, a name that was too German, too Hungarian, and too Jewish, and the first name unpronounceable to boot. So very early on, he signed his name Perlmuth, Eugene Perlmuth. Or perhaps an emigration official gave him that name on Ellis Island, perhaps it was an Irish cop who hated Eastern Europe and its citizens with German names who forced

2. Literally, "happy as God in France." *Trans.*

Uncle Jenö to change his name? Who knows. It's lucky he wasn't baptized O'Kennedy or O'Shaughnessy, or MacDonald or Pizza Hut or Vivendi Universal . . .

Uncle Eugene was a positive fellow, though, at any rate, the tenor of the times did not allow him to ask himself too many questions. He loved America, and America returned his love, since he became a millionaire there. That's what the family was saying in Szatmár and in Budapest. How many millions? And in which currency? In dollars or in pengös, or later on, in forints? Did anyone see his company's balance sheet? How about his tax returns? Who even knew anything about his company and the state of his wealth? Was that not an impression carefully nurtured by photographs, cigars, cars, Anglican women, and other gadgets that had the same effect on the family in Hungary as incense, guns, and glass beads once had on the natives at the time of the conquistadors? He married an English woman with a French name, Christine Beaufort, an Anglican. The family over there, in the old country couldn't understand it. Why all this circus, "Eugene" and "Perlmuth," and an English woman, an Anglican to boot (Anglican? What on earth is this? Are they anti-Semites too?). And "Christine," no kidding, a Perlmutter wife called Christine, does she wear a chain with a big gold cross between her two breasts? And on top of this, her name is French. What's going on with Jenö, Jenci? What is he running away from, leaving, trying to forget, to bury, to kill? Us? But, yet . . . he's a millionaire. The legend spreads, expands. Later on in Paris I tell all comers: my uncle in San Francisco, or rather my great-uncle, is on the list of the hundred wealthiest men in the United States.

In 1936, Eugene sends a gift to Budapest to his favorite

sister, my grandmother Blanka. It was a car, awesome-black-lacquered-varnished-waxed, what have you, the inside like a parlor, red leather armchairs, ashtrays, built-in bar, mahogany, two small lamps with lampshades . . . I remember so well the photo of the car, the chauffeur and his cap, the rest I can only imagine . . . I do remember the picture, but Uncle Eugene himself couldn't quite remember Hungary. What was his sister, a Budapest attorney's wife, to do with a car? No one knew how to drive it, and in that country at that time no one needed to know. He should have known. But how could he have known—he a poor wood merchant's orphan from Szatmár in Transylvania—how could he have known how the bourgeois of the capital, Budapest, were living? Or was it perhaps his way of taking revenge for his childhood?

*This car has been waiting for seventy years, waiting for me to tell about it, even though I'm not yet seventy myself, I'm the one and only, the sole and last person who can still tell about it before it disappears into the void unless . . . what, who? Me, me alone . . . Cars, things, anything, they're like people, just like them; they exist as long as someone remembers them. Only matter is stored in cemeteries. No cemetery, be it for humans or cars, can preserve memories. Only a human being's recollections can do so, through words, through speech. I am a living cemetery, yes, a living one, I'm alive and so are my dead, as long as I am. Hey you there, you know nothing. Just take a look at that box of photographs! You are glancing at it for the first time. I'm thinking without telling you that your attitude is a healthy one. It is easier for you to live without wallowing in a dead past. But in my case, it's the opposite, and it doesn't help me at all, not even to die, since I'm afraid of death. When I die, the red plastic fire truck that melted in the kitchen oven where I had placed it to put down the fire will die with me.*

*And so will the toy chemistry set my mother gave me, and the tricycle I left in front of the door when, I was abducted by a psychopath neighbor, and the book on the war of the animals, and my first novel, Mark Twain's* The Prince and the Pauper—*but others too have read this same novel—but no, no one read it like me, it's my reading of it that will die, and my gray sweater and my Russian camera that looked like a tank, and the* Lohndiener *of the hotel Austria in Vienna too will die along with me, the one Gabi and I drove crazy in 1956 by blocking the elevator in between two stories ten times a day, and the orange that was bought for me, also in Vienna around the same time, in December '56, the first whole orange I ate in my life because the one that my father succeeded in getting hold of in Budapest for Christmas of '54 had to be shared, the flesh between my mother and me while my father ate the inside of the skin.*

To come back to the car, according to my mother who remembered it and who often spoke of it to me, they only kept it for a few months. They had to hire a driver, they never knew where to go, before this they did their shopping on foot, everything was nearby, and anyway, they had a servant. So they invented various outings to keep the chauffeur busy: grandfather took my mother and my aunt to school, grandmother went shopping. Grandmother bought things she didn't need so as to use the car and give some work to the chauffeur, she who was more than economical, thrifty, niggardly, penny pinching, but couldn't stand to see this big fellow with his waxed moustache doing nothing all day long. One day, they said, enough is enough. They let the superb chauffeur go even though he was stylish, turned the wheel with majesty, opened and closed the door while holding his cap very elegantly in his gloved hand, either the left or the right one depending on which side, and they sold this black, waxed, scrubbed, honking, shining beast.

Cars must have been a powerful symbol in Uncle Eugene's life. Too bad I didn't know what my great-uncle's successive autos were: Chevrolets, Buicks, Oldsmobiles, Cadillacs, Studebakers, and even Hudsons. They would have been cause for so much talk, excitement, and wonderment.

*Hudsons were neither good nor beautiful but were much prized by the nomenklatura of the Hungarian Communist Party before it came into power. After the 1950s, the leaders no longer had a choice: they had to ride in ZIMs and in ZISs—did you know that M stood for Molotov and S for Stalin?*

A few days earlier, in a Parisian secondhand store, I had come across an old photograph (10 francs, it's such a deal . . . a deal? You must be kidding, for the photo of a stranger? It's sheer robbery!) showing a little boy pedaling at the wheel of a toy car, a little boy coiffed, Brylcreemed, smoothed out for the picture, with a small sweater and a small shirt—so stylish and so proper . . . This could never have been Uncle Eugene who absolutely didn't have a toy car in Szatmár, nor a white shirt like the little boy on the sepia photograph—but Eugene managed to catch up with the white shirts and particularly with cars.

At any rate, the automobile, this sumptuous gift, left a life-long impression on the family. Eugene came to visit in Budapest just once, right before World War II, accompanied by his wife who only spoke English and to whom no one had anything to say, though they were saying it anyway very politely with numerous hand kissing, heel clicking, and compliments in Hungarian, or in German, which she didn't understand either. But his visit left fewer memories and traces in the family's golden book than did the machine.

After the Communist takeover, my family as in the families of other survivors (of the war, the deportations—Nazi deportations first, and then the Communist ones—and emigration) would receive packages from their Western relatives. It was forbidden to send money, but allowed were tea, coffee, chocolate, nylon stockings, Maggi soup mixes, perfume . . . Uncle Eugene, or more precisely, Aunt Christine, would occasionally send parcels to these distant and practically unknown kin whose names she couldn't even remember. One of the parcels was addressed to "Felado." *Feladó* means "sender" in Hungarian; good old Christine had copied it from the back of one of the deliriously grateful letters—can you believe it! I am exhausted with laughter, and with sadness, and with shame. Shame because I, who has never known these American cousins, neither Eugene nor Christine, and who couldn't care less, had to work my buns off once a year to write them a letter to wish them happy New Year. At first in Hungarian, and then when I started to learn English, I had to compose my epistles in that language. These parcels were more than welcome and moreover, the whole family was waiting for a fabulous inheritance since Eugene didn't have children.

His brother Ernest, the Frenchman, had three of those, children that is . . . I do have to tell you everything, who else would do it? And if I didn't tell, all those people would be dead a second time, but then definitely so, and perhaps even God would forget them. At any rate, He did not remember them much, that is the Hungarian Jews of this century, blessed be He, and by the time He did remember them, they had already been turned into soap, lampshades, clouds, and it was too late.

When I was still in Budapest, I didn't know those children, over there, in France any more than I knew the American relatives, but I was never asked to write to those far-flung cousins of that branch of the family tree, and particularly not in French, a language I totally ignored. There was no inheritance to hope for, and they never sent even the smallest parcel of Maggi soup (or Knorr? I no longer remember) or razor blades (preferably Gillette, the best ones according to my father). This was all the more strange in that my mother went twice on vacation in Lille and Boulogne-sur-Mer with her cousins. Aunt Lucie, after Uncle Ernest's heroic death, had opened a fine lingerie shop in Lille, and it had made her well off—whence the little Rolex inserted with diamonds that was regularly repaired free of charge by the Genevan watchmaker. My mother's cousin married a writer. In the big photo album there is a portrait of the writer, and written on the back of the picture—I'm putting on my glasses and I read "Degrassi," "De Grassi," "de Grassi," "de Grasse" . . . I laugh again, but this time gladly: in this story, everyone keeps changing names.

And what of Uncle Eugene? He died, just like everyone did or will. He left all of his wealth to his wife, who felt it decent and proper to give some of it to his poor Hungarian relatives. I found a letter from the American lawyer addressed to my grandmother and listing the details of Uncle Eugene's possessions. There were a great number of stocks and bonds, a few properties in various California cities . . . he clearly was no Rockefeller. But still, it was not too shabby. And then for the humor of it: next to my aunt Christine's name, everywhere it appears, there is the name of a gentleman with a very English name . . . I don't understand it at all and so I'm sharing this detail without commenting on it. But by this time, we have come to know each other well enough (after so many pages filled with my happy vision of the world and of humanity) for you to be able to understand what lurks beneath the words . . . even with no word at all.

And thus, one day in 1958, my grandmother received a notice telling her that the sum she was due to receive from Aunt Christine from the will of her deceased brother Eugene was to be handed over to her in a form converted by the financiers of the People's Republic. This was to be a Java brand Czech motorcycle (it was no car: the bureaucrats had a petit bourgeois imagination and were used to thinking small). Grandmother felt it more reasonable to put the motorcycle up for sale rather than to learn to ride it at age sixty-nine. The brand new motorcycle stood for months at the entrance of the one room apartment on the third floor, this in a building without elevators.

I'm scratching my head. I am a survivor. A dinosaur from a time that no longer exists. And yet, in spite of it all, I don't feel that old. We have entered the third millennium, a cybernetic and interplanetary one, while I'm talking about Ellis Island, about Jewish emigrants, the 1905 San Francisco earthquake, the Dardanelles, memorial monuments, deportations, I who speak of fellows called stalin, hitler, stalin, hitler, lenin, mussolini . . . History, such an old story . . . photographs. That of Eugene and his small car: I only ever saw him in photos, yet what a role he played in my childhood!

Silence.

I miss my childhood. Well that's pretty typical, aren't we

all missing our childhood? But it is not the rotten world of the past that I'm missing, the war and its aftermath, hitlerism, misery and politics, and the absence of any politics, and of any future, and the presence of no future—you can well imagine that I wouldn't miss that . . . I don't care about the country of my childhood, about that world. And besides, I hail from nowhere. Those who, like me, have three passports, can either be proud of it and feel rich and safe, or feel utterly and definitely lost. I belong to this second group.

And yet . . . I do miss me. I miss the child me. The child of before, of before it, of where before was. The past is indeed truly a foreign country. My country was a family, one that included the names of the dead, memories, stories about the American uncle, the parcels—that childhood. It was like all childhoods, but it was mine. That country will not come back, it's as if it never existed.

# 7

# Józsi

He was to haunt me all my life. I'm told I take after him. In what way? Two or three small details: he loved art, women, onions and tomatoes, and he smoked cigars and the pipe. I no longer smoke. But fundamentally? How am I to know?

I was only three years old when Józsi died in those atrocious circumstances, and the only memory I retain of him—just like the memory of the gas factory and the bun linking me to my grandfather—belongs in the ordinariness of everyday life. I am on my way to the bathroom, I assume I asked

for help because he told me: "you're big enough now to go by yourself."

I own many of his paintings. I, who longs to own nothing, am clinging to these paintings. I feel as if I am the repository of . . . a duty. A rescue mission. Let *this* remain of him, at least.

Józsi was in fact an art historian, specializing in baroque art, particularly that of Transylvania. But he was also a historian in a larger sense. He studied the castles and the churches of his native province and wrote numerous monographs about them. As a result, Józsi, a Jewish high school principal's son, lived in the proximity, the entourage and perhaps even the friendship of nobles, nabobs, magnates, prince whatshisname, Count B., Count T., the primate of Esztergom, etc. . . .

*Oh God! How I hate their guts!*
*She reads this over my shoulder in Paris in 2002, there's a feel-*

ing of peace, almost of happiness, and she tells me, "you are putting in too much of yourself. It's a book you're writing. You should keep some distance." I reply that I don't want to. It's too important, it's too locked in, embedded, buried. I tell her that I don't know the boundary between literature and nonliterature. I must be involved. It must come out. Hatred rises in me like an urge to vomit. Why is it so strong? They have never harmed me, these Hungarian aristocrats of whom I never met a single one in person. But I hate their world, that world, that of princes, bishops, bishop-princes . . . It's also that of the haves sitting on their asses, also the world of peasant leaders, of beer drinkers and would-be remakers of the world, of the Stammtisch—the regulars's table at the fancy café, the world of those who are from somewhere and who state it, who trumpet it, who impose their superiority, and mostly take profit and advantages from it. I bear my "foreignness"—displaced, alien, several times naturalized, a Jew to the end. Since I first wrote this, I came across a 1972 text of a Brassens song that delighted me: "that chauvinistic race, wrapped in the flag . . . bombarding your ears about their native country till they hurt. Imbeciles happy to have been born somewhere."[1] This is where the difference lies: for his salvation, Józsi needed these nobles of his home province, of their home province, to be able to study their dwellings from the inside while the counts barons princes prímás, needed him for their glory. (The head of the Hungarian Church and the first violin of a Tzigane band are both called prímás: hercegprímás and cigányprímás. Perhaps they are secretly competing to find out who is the better cymbalom player?)

Bíró József, nicknamed Józsi or Jóska, was my father's younger brother. He was the darling, the favorite son who

1. The original French text of Brassens's song: "La race des chauvins, des porteurs de cocardes . . . qui vous font voir du pays natal jusqu'à loucher. Les imbéciles heureux qui sont nés quelque part." *Trans.*

succeeded in everything. My father succeeded too (in medicine, all the way to the Academy) but he had to work at it. They said that everything came easy for József. He died at age thirty-eight; at the time I'm writing now, he might still be alive. They live to a ripe old age in my family, that is, those allowed to suffer—in their mind and their spirit—from the ravages of time. He would be ninety-three years old now, and probably senile. His intellect and capacity for work were way above average. At home we had several monumental theses each signed with a different name (of one noble or another) that had all been written by him for money, in addition to his own two theses, one in the field of the history of art on Transylvanian baroque castles, the other on Coptic and Aramaic languages. (I was told he knew them perfectly . . . do people still speak Aramaic, write it?) Among his other books there is a remarkable *History of European Painting.* In addition to his historical work, he was also a talented painter. When I see paintings by his Hungarian contemporaries sold at auction, I can see how beautifully he painted, often better than the others who were known, admired, and celebrated. He was still searching for his own style. His large painting representing the Plaza of the Franciscans in Budapest, was perhaps his masterpiece and reconstructs perfectly the Parisian atmosphere of a painting by Marquet. József painted in it a small black car with a bluish roof that might have even been thought to be a copy, that is only if he had had the opportunity to see Marquet's paintings, but he never left Hungary (and what if it was Marquet who had copied József?). Some other of his works are reminiscent of Munch and the German expressionists—and he painted my father with eyes of stone, in the stern pose and with the black suit of Rembrandt's Dr. Tulp. I worship his pictorial work—"worship" is not too strong a word here. I appreciate it for sentimental reasons (his tragic death) as well as selfish ones (what if I really do resemble him?). He was a hard worker, a ladies man—a successful one; he studied, wrote, painted; he was a *Lebenskünstler,* an artist and enjoyer of life. Too bad for me, but it's too late. And if he was not like I'm describing him, this is nonetheless the image I have of him based on various accounts.

He only got married once, toward the end of his life: just before the war, he married one of his women friends, the very beautiful and intelligent and cultured Auer Anikó. I've been told this was in order to use his own privileged status to protect her. He had been granted a status of exemption in consideration of his work for and on Transylvania, still a "sensitive zone" because it had been recently taken back from the Romanians: the laws affecting the Jews did not apply to Józsi, and this exception protected his close family as well: his parents and his wife (Józsi and his father thus were killed by mistake . . .).

But, thanks to Józsi, Anikó survived. She left Hungary as soon as the war ended and went first to Switzerland, then to Stockholm, where she became a bookseller at Nordiska Bokhandeln, never remarried and cursed Hungary forever. She helped me after I left, often sent me money and used of her influence to get me my first job in publishing. When she was seventy-five, she met one of the loves of her youth and she moved in with him in Vienna, but without marrying because she wanted to remain Bíró Józsefné, Mrs. József Bíró, till her death. In 1992, I participated in organizing an exhibition of Bíró József in Budapest. On this occasion, Anikó came back to her native city for the first time since the war. She was wearing a big golden medallion she had received from the hands of the king of Sweden for having courageously worked thirty years? Forty years? Two hundred years? . . . in the same Nordic bookstore on the street of the princess.

She came to see me in Geneva, and we took the boat tour. The weather was lovely on the richest lake in the world. Pretty young women in slacks were leaning on the rail. "Did you see that pretty ass?" she suddenly asked me (I had seen it).

Anikó inquired if I could, during one of my brief (always brief) visits to Budapest, pick up a parcel that had been kept sealed with her name on it at my father's home since the war. I picked it up and then called her in Stockholm. She told me to open it, she said, so as to check its content. There were about fifty photographs of her naked, a splendid young woman in all sorts of daring poses, romantic, lascivious, prurient, and frankly pornographic . . . Can you imagine at the times, the early 1940s in Budapest, in Eastern Europe! Are you aware of the prudery, the moral and sexual hypocrisy of those years, in that place? I was troubled, intrigued, excited and startled in the face of this intimacy, these images, and even more by the desire of a lady now in her sixties who asked me to be the spectator, the voyeur, of her past splendor and freedom. She asked me what I thought of them. I was twenty-eight years old at the time. What I thought of them . . .

All those pictures were taken by Józsi, as were those I discovered later in a drawer after my father's death. They featured a spectacular golden blond woman with long flowing hair, dressed in various elegant and sophisticated outfits in thirties style. On some photos, her hands were hidden in an enormous fur muff. The pictures were all posed, all affected, all artificial, all smiling. On a dozen of "artistic" photographs, she is in a swimming suit beneath cascading water at the pool, in a sexy, innocent pose, one arm raised, one hip jutting out just like a starlet. The photos are smaller than Anikó's but it is evident that the same eyes were looking through the shutter. On one, there's the inscription "Maryvonne." There was no one in Hungary by that name, she must have been French. There were at least fifty pictures. Józsi must have been very much in love with this cinematographic beauty, who too, was lavishing loving smiles to the camera—to the person holding the camera? How did they talk to each other? Józsi was deaf, like my father but more so and was affected at an earlier age. And I'm sure that even though he might have been speaking Coptic and Aramaic, he did not speak French.

Spring of 2001: I'm in Budapest, on the Pest side, in front of the Lánchíd bridge support, a bridge also known as the "chain bridge." It's a beautiful day, the May sun is shining, there's a gentle breeze. I love this kind of weather, I've always loved it—this caressing sun and wind. A couple is strolling, arms around each other. The young woman drops a book, the man bends down and picks it up.

One of Maryvonne pictures was taken in Budapest, on one of the Danube quays. The young woman is smiling, she is obviously blooming and happy—just as, I imagine Józsi, the photographer, must be. I'm sure of this because a photograph is a two-sided mirror. In the background, behind the blonde, there is the support of the suspended bridge on the Pest side.

It is at this precise spot that, shortly after, Józsi was shot and thrown into the river.

# 8

## Nándor

Nándor was another of the family's *Lebenskünstlers*. There was yet another, Hegedüs Géza, one of my father's cousins on his mother's side.

*While writing this, I realize that I know very few of my father's relatives on his father's side, and they haven't played the same role in my life as his relatives on his mother's side. Could this be because of social, class factors? On one side there were the Nagyvárad bourgeois, merchants, who had been there for centuries while, on the other, were villagers, teachers, who had migrated to town ...*

Hegedüs Nándor was born Hirschl Nándor, but like all his brothers, he "Magyarized" his family name. My grandmother kept Hirschl. This might make you laugh, or at least crack a bit of a smile, because before Magyarizing its name, the family was forced to "Germanize" it. During Joseph II's reign, between 1780 and 1790, the Jews of the empire were forced to adopt German names regardless of where they lived. The German "Hirschl" comes from the Jewish "Herschel." Herschel Spiro, my great-great . . . in short, my ancestor who was the only Jewish merchant who had stayed in Nagyvárad

when the Turks were kicked out (along with the Jews, I'm inferring, but I could be wrong. This fact, like so many others, would require verification—but that's not what I do). History did keep a written trace of the event somewhere (I don't know where but Géza who was the one who told me about it and who is dead will gladly tell you): Herschel Spiro lived in Nagyvárad in 1694. This is why my father could write me one day that our family was one of the oldest Jewish families in Transylvania.

*He also wrote it in the official request he sent to his country's authorities in 1940 or 1942 to ask them to not dispossess him of his right to vote and his Hungarian citizenship. The crypto-fascist government dispossessed him anyway, and then, a few years later, another government of the same country wrote him that it had been an error and had been illegal. My father and grandmother left Transylvania, and I later on left Hungary, thus bringing to a close the story of the Herschel-Hirschl-Hegedüs of Nagyvárad—the end of a history.*

Nándor was an artist of life by vocation and by necessity: vocation because of his talents and inclinations, and necessity because his wife Paula (said to be very beautiful) died young, well before the war, of a grave illness, and Nándor, then a young widower, made good use of his remaining time by living to live.

While I owe the construction of my self, my emotional structure, and my most salient character traits to my mother, I owe my intellectual development to my father, to Nándor, and to Géza. It's Nándor (I used to call him Nándika) who gave me my first grown up book, my first novel, the Mark Twain I mentioned earlier.

*It's May of 2001 and I'm in Budapest. While browsing in a used book store, I come across a very old Hungarian translation of Mark Twain's* The Prince and the Pauper. *Nostalgic and sentimental as always, I buy it. I discover that the editor-printer is this same Tolnai whose printing presses had so often rocked my childhood sleep at number 12, Dohány Street, in the building where my grandparents used to live. When I return in August, the printing business is gone. The whole of the building has been demolished-rebuilt, uglyfied-transformed into offices that are for rent. We are drinking coffee across the street from that building and at the foot of another building where grandmother Bíró and Nándor used to live. This café did not exist in the "olden days" (as senior citizens are wont to say). I look at the building and feel nothing. Anni and my mother, who both lived there in their youth along with Nándor and all of my grandparents, have been dead for a long time . . . What can I say? We have to accept time. Or even rejoice: also seated at my table is Y. who is only twenty-one years old . . .*

It's also Nándor who, the first after my father, talked to me about politics, literature, journalism, theater . . . This requires rectification and explanation. First: he wasn't speaking to me about all this, but to my father. I was much too young. I didn't count, they never spoke to me . . . but I was listening. Nándor would come for afternoon coffee once a week, on Thursdays, I seem to recall. He was a polyglot and spoke just about all the "useful" languages (as everyone knows, "useful" languages are all Western European, the ones spoken by the *Herrenvölker*, the noble peoples), plus Romanian. He was working in the news agency of the Hungarian state, a sinecure. He wasn't actually required to put in an appearance at the office, and he was among the lucky few who were allowed to travel. He thus had all the leisure (though not so much the tranquility of mind, which the times did not allow for) to write his articles and his books, to run after women, and to alternate his discussion sessions between Géza and my father. His culture was immense (like my father's), so their discussions fascinated me: they brought up politicians, poets, writers, history. (They never spoke of the fine arts. This is strange: Józsi, the pride of the family, was a painter and moreover, the two brothers couldn't hear very well, which should have oriented their conversations toward the visual arts . . . I must say that music was never discussed at home; we didn't even have a record player and only my mother listened to the news on the radio—which got her into trouble when a neighbor denounced her for listening to the French radio.)

The matters under discussion were approached from a personal angle. Both my father and uncle were Freemasons, and as such, members of the Radical party (joint membership in the two organizations was taken for granted) and personally knew several politicians. My father, already hard of hearing, seldom frequented these groups, but Nándor did, particularly in the period immediately following the war when the outward appearance of democracy still led to the belief in a future political life, a parliament, and elections. Moreover, before the war, Nándor had played a certain political role in Transylvania (I am repeating myself). He was a deputy representing the Hungarian minority in the Romanian parliament in Bucharest. And, I just read in a Hungarian paper that he was still "somebody" after the war: undersecretary of information in the coalition government just before the Communist takeover. Moreover, he also belonged to the Freemason elite: while my father, in great part

because of his hearing problem, remained a simple "brother," his uncle was Great Orator of Hungary.

*Don't ask me what this means. My relationship with the Freemasonry
is ambiguous. I am such an anarchist, proud to be a neithergodnor-
master-ist since always, but particularly since I left their country of
organizations-groups-cells-associations-unions-clubs-party—what,
party? The Party!—the whole submitted and completely controlled.
I am signed up nowhere, I belong to nothing, I resist all and any alle-
giances and submissions. But my father's family is a family of Masons:
almost all the men, my grandfather Márk, great master of a lodge in
his town, my father and Nándor. There's only Géza, Józsi, and me who
. . . I thus feel affection for these Masons. I can't help liking their ideas,
the ideas they defended in Hungary. They were optimistic, innocents
and unaware democrats. My father told me that, besides great intellectual joy, his membership had brought him nothing, neither privi-
lege, nor work, nor money, nor any position, nor help or assistance,
and that, at least for Hungary, the infamous Masonic solidarity was a
myth . . . I can still see my father pace for hours, and I mean hours, in
his room, always on the same part of the rug, which over time, because
of this decade long frantic marching, lost its colors. What he was doing was learning by heart and rehearsing the lectures he was going to
present to his "brothers." Goethe and the natural sciences, Napoleon
and medicine, Helmholtz . . . The lecture on Lavoisier ended as follows:
"Stand up proud scholar and tax collector, prepare yourself for death,
allonzanfandölápátri."[1] My father was a brilliant orator and a re-*

1. This is the opening line of the *Marseillaise*, the French national anthem,
which translated into English states, "Let us go, children of the fatherland."
The line is in French but the words are crunched together into a single word
and the spelling is Hungarian. This sounds hilarious to a French readership
but, unfortunately, it cannot be rendered into English. *Trans.*

*markable talker but he was simply not able to respond to questions he couldn't hear. Masonry was forbidden in Hungary under rákosi as it had already been under horthy, and of course under every dictator-ships, pétain-hitler & co. The clandestine membership met informally in a café—on certain evenings my father went to the Kárpátia Café —I was confused, my father never went to cafés. Years later, when I was already an adult, I found out that it was there that the "brothers" met. As to the lectures . . . ? I don't know. When my father died, I found in the hidden corners of his linen closet his Masonic insignia which I had never seen, neither at home nor elsewhere: an apron, various metal instruments . . . Two mafia-type real estate agents were there when I discovered them. One of the agents asked me for them for "the Free-masonry museum." Even though I thought this must be a lie as there was no such museum in Hungary, I gave them to this crook. Even if he resells them, particularly if he resells them, they will be in the hands of people who find them important—and they will at least remain in their home, in Hungary.*

But, to come back to Nándor. Before the war he was a jour-nalist, then editor-in-chief of a very influential newspaper in Nagyvárad, and in that capacity, he formed close relation-ships with the major authors of the time. I will not bore you with unknown, unpronounceable names, which nonethe-less make my heart and the hearts of my fellow Hungar-ians flutter. I will only mention the divine Ady, the greatest Hungarian poet of the twentieth century, who was working in the same office as Nándor. The war and the paper having been lost, Nándor also went for afternoon coffee at the home at his other nephew Géza, a novelist, playwright, professor of the history of the theater at the university, and the friend of all the writers of his generation, as well as of all the actors (and lover of a great number of student actresses and future divas). After his newspaper closed, Nándor found consolation in writing about the authors of his time he had known, and particularly about Ady. But at Géza's house, he automatically got to know the new Hungarian intellectual generation.

It would be wrong for me to so quickly skip over Géza who also contributed to my education. He was the author of more than sixty novels and countless radio plays, of literary and theatrical works of popularization, of poetry books and even of translations (I believe he did speak Latin but it might have been Greek to him, or vice versa). His writing bulimia, his successful "graphomania," also manifested itself in the rest of his life: strong drinks, tobacco, women . . . He still managed to last more than eighty years. Since he lived at my grandparents while in high school, he became Józsi's best friend, and he remained very closed to my father, and then to both my parents. I was the only child around him to be interested in the same things he was: not yet women, nor alcohol or tobacco in all its forms, but strongly by literature. Thus he spoke often to me about it. Then after a span of time when he was not writing (he was the executive director of a protest publishing house during the thaw of 1955, then during the revolution of '56), he became one of the country's most popular writers—though I'm not saying one of the best—and consequently one of the richest. Summer of '56, in his country house of Visegrád, on the shore of the Danube, I met everyone who was worth meeting: famous authors newly freed from prison, talented poets suddenly allowed to publish . . .

*That summer of '56, when all of Budapest was preparing for the revolution that broke out in October, particularly marked me with my first heartbreak caused by a very beautiful brunette, older than I, and who chose more experienced people for her first frolics. She was seen bathing naked with Swabian boys in the Danube on the very evening I waited for her in front of the house, my hair combed, dressed to the nines in a very white white shirt. The next day, Géza, seeing me despondent, told me: "Go ahead, cry, it will make you feel better. You're lucky. There's nothing better than heartbreak and femmes fatales, or even hysterical ones. It makes you feel alive." I did listen to the old fart but it's only decades later that I came to understand what he meant. Pity the one who has not suffered from love. (I wrote and published this story in French when I was an adult. The girl in question read it in Budapest and then wrote to me. She was unhappy and felt herself to be ugly, fat, swollen up with alcohol. She had cried when reading that she had been beautiful, seductive, attractive, free, young. I didn't answer. Then I found out that she was an advanced alcoholic and she had committed suicide.)*

Half (well, to be nice, let's say one-fourth) of Géza's stories, of the people he'd seen, the events he participated in or witnessed . . . were untrue. But this is of no import . . . My first memory of this short fat man, plagued with tics, exaggerating his 'r' sounds, a nonstop smoker of cigarettes, cigars, and pipes, is linked to the arrival at our home in 1946, of a starving young man wearing only long very dirty underpants and a waiter's jacket. This was Géza. He had been a forced member of a disciplinary company (as a Jew and communist, he couldn't have been more suitable!) and had been dragged by the Hungarian army and then by the German and finally by the Russian one all the way to Siberia, from where it took him a year to get back to Budapest. The first thing he found out was that his house had been destroyed. Then my parents told him that his father and mother had been gassed.

He did not show up at my mother's funeral, and then it was his turn to die, and my father accompanied him to the cemetery. I went by his house and saw that the city of Budapest had put a huge black marble plaque in his memory next to the entrance.

As a kid, I clung to my elders' every word—including Nándor's, Géza's, and my father's—while they were sipping their coffee with milk (and eating bread slices spread with goose fat and paprika). I gobbled up all of their opinions on novelists and on past and present kings, on poets, and on actors. I filled myself with biographical details and anecdotes. They never said anything off color—was it because I was there? And yet Nándor didn't temper his words to say what was on his mind. One day when I was six years old (this is important), I asked him why he didn't marry his then girlfriend, F. Juliska. I can still hear his answer and see his ramrod bearing: "Because I'm not mad!"—without any other comment.

He also spoke to me about foreign countries (I didn't leave Hungary till I was fifteen, except for a trip to Romania, to Nagyvárad), about foreigners, also about the war—who didn't talk about the war in Hungary in the '40s, and even the '50s, and even the '60s, and even now? As an undersecretary of state, he attended a peace conference in Geneva (was it still the League of Nations, or already the UN? I should check, but is it of import? It doesn't fall within my project. I can speak of my family, but not of the world. And yet . . . wasn't the League of Nations killed by hitler and mussolini?) And then, in the midst of all this, he represented the Hungarian Masonic lodge at a Masonic conference in Paris in 1947.

*Geneva, Paris . . . Ten years later I lived here, twenty years later, there. Along with Budapest, these cities have become the three poles of my existence.*

Nándor always dressed with old fashioned elegance; even during the stalinist years. He wore a coat with a fur collar and leggings (instead of stalinist we should rather say: *rákosist*—to be pronounced *rakoshit*[2]—the name of the Hungarian dictatoriculus, dictatorinet, the very bloody *rákosi mátyás*, "the great Comrade Stalin's best student").

I saw Nándor again thirteen years later in Basel, where he was visiting his only son. He was coming from Paris where he had been invited to a dinner party given by some French people, in honor of a Hungarian who was passing through— I don't know who he was, these people are always passing through.

Nándor told the story while we were seated at the family table in Basel:

"Our hosts wanted to please this Hungarian by inviting other Hungarians. In Paris. He had come specifically for this. Only for this. From Budapest. Sixteen hundred kilometers just to see other Hungarians. Everyone was very elegant, especially elegant. Among the guests was a Hungarian actor very famous in Hungary. What's-his-name, you know him too, Ádám.

2. The French version has another pun, "*rákosien*—to be pronounced *racochien*," involving the combination of a rack and a dog, which of course wouldn't have worked in English. But my solution does render some of the spirit of the original. *Trans.*

"This actor regularly spent several months in Paris. He spoke French with very few mistakes but with a marked accent, which limited him to playing foreigners.

"'Can you imagine! I am Hamlet in the National Theater in Budapest, and the prince of Homburg, and Faust, but here, I only play old Jews. Because of my accent. These idiots Parisians can't tell the difference between accents, they think that all Eastern European accents are Jewish. And even that is meaningless. The French only know of Polish Jews. For them, all the inhabitants of Eastern Europe have a Polish Jewish accent. Me, I do know how to pronounce *u*. I don't say *ri de Tirenne* instead of *rue de Turenne* like the Polacks (laughter around the table)—but it doesn't matter because I roll my *r*. That's all it takes with the French. They think all the people from Eastern Europe roll their *r*'s. So that does it. I have to specialize playing little old men who survived the camps. They put wrinkles, make up on me. I bend, I have tics, as for the accent, I exaggerate it, I make it Polish, but no director is aware of this, they have never gone any farther east than Tokio, Sofia, Warsaw, kif-kif. As to Budapest, they think it's another pronunciation of Bucharest. But I'm accepting, what else can I do if I want to make a nest here? Except that I'm afraid of remaining stuck in this character. I am not anti-Semitic, well, at least no more so than other Hungarians, but I'm fed up with only playing Jews—and particularly old Jews. When I go back to Hungary, I play Romeo, Lorenzaccio, the Cid, in Hungarian, and without accent, and I am young and handsome and stand straight! I want to play Hamlet at the Comédie-Française! After all he is a Dane described by a Brit, so surely he is entitled to a bit of an accent . . . or perhaps Prince Mychkine, at least he rolled his *r*'s . . .'

"No one answered him, neither the other Hungarians who were present, nor the dead Jews who were absent. But me, I thought that for once there was an immanent justice that punished the actor where the others had sinned, which made him pay for them all. It was a mythical, or Dantesque fate that forced the representative of the Jew-eaters to play Jewish roles for all eternity, and if he was ever allowed to interpret Hamlet, this Hamlet would have to be, unavoidably because of his fate and his punishment, a Kafkaesque Jew, but one wearing white stockings, a black caftan, and side curls under his fur *schtraimel*, uncertain, hesitant, tortured by doubts, overwhelmed with confusion, while the director, a goy of course, would ask him, in order to make the character credible, to emphasize his *yiddishkeit* and speak with a Polish accent."

Nándor's only child, Bódi, attended university in Switzerland thanks to his father. He had been sent there by his father, funded by his father, his life saved by his father. He stayed in Basel, married a Swiss woman of Czech origin, had a career in one of the big chemical companies of which he was head engineer at the time. I stayed with them for ten days at the same time as Nándor. One evening, when Nándor was out, they very formally requested I come to their living room where they asked me to tell Nándor to not spit on the lawn and to put his socks away in his room.

*But now Bódi too is dead. The love of order doesn't make one immortal. I asked his wife, when I learned of his death, which language he spoke on his deathbed after spending sixty years in the German speaking part of Switzerland. I already knew the answer. I let you guess.*
*That's the way it goes.*

When I saw Nándor again, in 1967, he was a shrunken old man who no longer talked about women or travels or actors. He was living in that gloomy apartment with my grandmother and was ailing. He told K., the horrible thing about old age is that you want to cry all the time.

And then, at the end, a farce: when, after Nándor's funeral (my grandmother was already dead), Bódi wanted to collect some of his father's things and get rid of the apartment, the maid showed him a marriage certificate. She had convinced Nándor, who was more than eighty years old, to marry her so she could live in the apartment, not to own it but only for the right to rent it.

When I had my father buried next to his mother, I had to have the tomb opened and, to my surprise, I found an urn containing Nándor's ashes. No one remembered it.

# 9

# Anni

This is where we encounter misfortune, but in this case, that misfortune did not result from collective History but from individual history.

How is it that the most spoiled child, the most adored, the youngest who had been so desired, the preferred one, the most gifted, the one who could dance so graciously, and who wanted to be an actress, how is it that such a beautiful young woman came to be so unhappy and, particularly, how is it that she lived and died alone? (Because she was a Jew in the 1930s in Hungary she was not allowed to study theater,

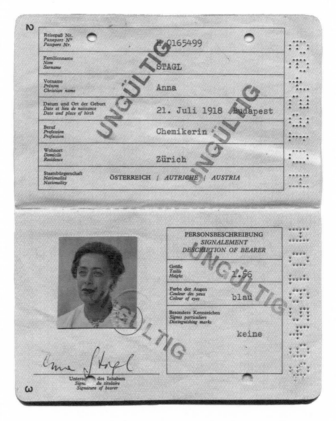

but Anni still managed to become somebody: a chemical engineer. Hungary can take pride in being the first country in Europe, even before Germany, to establish a *numerus clausus*, a quota against Jews. On September 2, 1920, the morning after the start of school, which traditionally happens on September 1 in Hungary, a certain Haller—no! no capital letter for this pig—haller istván, the minister of culture, proudly announced to the parliament: "We are the very first to plan on voting this sort of law in.")

I have given a lot of thought to Anni's mysterious existence. Everything fated my mother's only sister to be the happiest, the most fulfilled: her looks, the love of her parents, her entourage's admiration, her education...

Courted by handsome, intelligent, promising young men —a poet, a chemist, a doctor—she quickly married after the war the emptiest big mouth, her great love, a social-democrat leader. And when he fled to Israel just before the Communist takeover, she followed him there. This marked the beginning of her long fall into the tighter and tighter knots of misfortune that were to last till her miserable death, a kind of suicide with her lungs filled with water, in my arms, in a gloomy Zurich hospital forty years later.

She yearned for children but she didn't have any. Instead she had to contend with an unfaithful and compulsively jealous husband who had her watched and guarded by a German sheepherder who hated everyone.

In Israel she didn't learn Hebrew. In Vienna, then in Bern, then in Zurich she only poorly learned German and not at all the Swiss-German dialect she would have needed when she left Israel for Switzerland where she started to work as a cleaning lady. The lawyer for whom she worked fired her when he found out she had advanced degrees because. He said, he couldn't afford the luxury of having a Ph.D. in chemistry as a maid. This forced her to get hold of herself and start working as a chemist again.

She was neither intelligent nor a hard working student, and contrary to what I believed for a long time, her failures had already started while she was in elementary school. She had always been described both by her parents and herself as a brilliant student when attending primary and secondary school, and then university. She was held as an example in contrast to my mother described as a hopeless duncette (does this word exist? It's too good to pass up). After her death I discovered that her school notebooks already showed the warning flashes of a catastrophic learning odyssey. But I wouldn't blame her for it.

Anni distrusted everybody, and nurtured an irrational but noisy disgust toward

*Israel (and its inhabitants)*
*Hebrew (ancient, modern, and in between)*
*Arabs (and their language)*
*Swiss-Germans (and their dialect)*
*Hungarians*

And this was not all. When I inadvertently let her know that, for a short time, I had a girlfriend from Reunion Island, she warned me seriously that our children were going to be green. And she was so ashamed—but of what exactly? Of everything: of Hungary, of Israel . . . of herself, so much so that when she arrived in Switzerland she had false papers made claiming she was Venezuelan. This was all the easier to claim in that Anni didn't speak a word of Spanish. Then she entered into a sham marriage[1] for which she paid good money to an Austrian named Stagl whom she met only once, at the city hall—so as to be neither Hungarian, nor Israelite . . . perhaps so as not to be, at all.

Anni worshipped the Hungarian culture of the past, her family, her mother, her father, my mother, me, her sole nephew—as long as she didn't have to be in personal contact with them, with us—and also the mythical founder of Migros, the Swiss department stores chain for which she worked, a certain Dutweiler, or Duttweiler, or Dutweyler, the humanist inventor of frantic low cost shopping (the prices being of course in Swiss francs). She used to shower me with gifts. She had settled in Switzerland to "take care of me"—but, *Gott sei dank,* she didn't find work in Geneva, the city where I lived, so this forced her to practice her love-admiration through the intermediary of food parcels. I accepted them with pleasure but without expressing any gratefulness, which I absolutely didn't feel. Since I had managed to escape from motherly love, I had no desire to become

1. The French version makes a play on words that cannot be translated into any English equivalent: "Puis elle s'est fait épouser (en blanc! je veux dire; un mariage non pas en blanc mais blanc . . . pour de l'argent au noir)." In French a sham marriage is referred to as white and under-the-table money is referred to as black, as in "black market" in English. So the pun states she had a wedding not in white, but white, and paid black money for it.

an aunt's affective slave. She wrote letters to my mother that were burning with sentiments and sentimentality. My mother, on her part, was jealous of her and reproached her for having been her parents' favorite . . . even as she reproached me for not loving my aunt who had done so much for me. (At that time, it was her favorite conversation topic, thus hinting to her deep feeling of guilt toward her sister.) My mother forced me to make gifts in turn to Anni, to send her money "to survive." Each time they met, in Switzerland or Budapest, they always and immediately got mad at each other, with screams, slammed doors, frantic aimless walking for hours, and threats of bilateral suicide. Anni has always taken care to stage her arrivals; she disembarked with pomp and ceremonies, with her famous gray suitcases (in imitation crocodile) filled with useless and often defective gifts (blouses with a single sleeve, stained pajamas, useless and incomprehensible electric gadgets . . . it was her job to test new products for Migros).

The state of her finances couldn't have been as disastrous as my mother liked to think. Indeed, during the last ten years of Anni's life she participated in organized, solitary travels (in with a group of strangers—how horrible!), to far-away Australia, California, Thailand, and from where she sent me superkitschy postcards and brought me back matching gifts in colored or golden plastic imitation bamboo and ivory . . .

Mistrust of people, apparent fear of men, unfounded feelings of superiority, superficial and scattered culture . . . My grandparents, blinded by admiration for their youngest daughter didn't do her any favor with the way they raised her. Spoiled rotten, adored and worshiped, her upbringing, the one we all need to become a human being able to face life, was a total failure. Her lawyer father was the one who demanded, pleaded by letter for Anni's divorce in Haifa, and obtained it—all the way from Budapest, five thousand kilometers away. And this in opposition to the expressed desire and wishes of the interested parties, the spouses. It is this sort of upbringing that my mother attempted—but dictatorial love didn't work on me.

Here's a photographic memory flash. One day a whole bunch of Hungarian cousins showed up at Anni's apartment in Seebach (you know the place? Seebach the lake resort? Seebach the river-by-the-sea resort? Seebach the waterworks resort? Glamorous, sexy, trendy suburb of Zurich? You mean you never went there? It's not too late. This place keeps on existing by changing it's facade to fool the hunter . . . ). There is not enough room in the small studio apartment, there are at least six of us engaging in a more and more lively discussion, "I'll sleep here, no, I will," but my aunt wanted ab-so-lu-te-ly to sleep on the balcony, I love this, I'm used to it, don't bug me, the weather is too great to sleep locked up in an apartment, it's my apartment, so I'm the one who decides . . . In the end, night and fatigue made us give up. Everyone gets to sleep where they can, Anni on an outdoor lounge chair on the balcony . . . The next day, the group continues their journey toward Geneva, and I'm alone with my aunt. "Can you imagine," she says, "these young people let me sleep on the balcony."

Another memory: her visit to Paris at our home. Two weeks (perhaps it was only one, but interminable). Anni, today is K.'s birthday, I'm taking you out to a restaurant. First argument: OK but I'm paying. After the usual first ten minutes of yelling, we pass on to the next topic: where shall we go? For her, Anni insists, anything, anything will do. But really, you must have a preference . . . No, none. The two of you should choose. I'm just happy to be with you. So we decide on a Chinese restaurant whose cuisine has an excellent reputation. Would you like this? Of course. On the way back, Anni who had remained silent, finally opens her mouth: I hate Chinese food.

After helping her on her deathbed (oh, but this is a falsehood: we die alone, without help. So I should rather say, after I was present at her death, after I wiped her brow, held her hand real tight when she told me at the last moment in Hungarian, "that's it"), I had to empty her apartment in this deadly suburb of this deadly city smiling at death. It took me three full days. I first slept at a friend's house, this was a help but after two days, she kicked me out . . . I didn't understand why . . . I must have smelled of death. I went to a hotel to sleep with my dead. In my aunt's apartment there were hundreds of fuzzy pictures of the view from her window taken with a lousy Polaroid camera (perhaps even a thousand, I didn't count them. I just threw them all in the trash). The small suburban houses in the distance; the belfry of a church, the sky, clouds, the neighborhood lawn under the snow, the street . . . not a single human being. And then all of the issues of the Zurich daily paper to which she had a subscription, piled up everywhere, for years, under the bed, in the cabinets, on the closets . . . I put everything in a very large number of plastic garbage bags, along with purses, and net bags for groceries, and suitcases (the gray suitcases in imitation crocodile). When the bin in the street was full, I piled up the rest in front of the door of the building, something that was strictly forbidden under threat of a fine, this in writing on a very elegant and classy metal plaque. I felt intense jubilation as I did it: do open up these bags, *Messieurs* the guardians of order/ly trash,[2] as is your right and habit. Search into the garbage bags for a name on a letter, a bill, the name of the culprit, do ring her bell after the garbage truck refused to take all those illegal bags piled up haphazardly in a forbidden place . . . After several weeks of negotiations and investigation, the Helvetic constabulary, unable to find the author of the crime, the criminal herself, and under pressure from the building's tenants, had to resign itself to be the one to take away all this detritus of a life that had absconded illegally . . . I wish I could have been there! Besides this, there was nothing of value, no jewelry of any worth, only cheap plastic junk—just like my mother's, except that my mother owned an apartment and a cottage by the Danube. Anni, the tenant of a tiny two room apartment . . . well, we don't seem to be doing too well. What would the anti-Semites have to say about this?

I had her incinerated, according to her wishes. I asked a rabbi to preside, a rabbi I had picked out from the phone book, a rabbi whom she had never seen, and who did not know her. He asked me a few questions about her, I answered and then he said the usual prayers (he didn't seem to believe in them, I can assure you) in front of five people, K., three unknown old ladies her ex-colleagues, and me. He didn't say one word about Anni, not one personal word, no sermon, no farewell, he tried to get me to speak but I refused. I was too

2. The French pun reads "gardiens de l'ord(u)re . . ." so that *ordre* (order) is encompassed in *ordure*, which means "trash."

moved, almost in tears, I couldn't have said one word. I paid him in cash, which made him very happy. He even told me, perfect, cash! . . . He didn't have to declare it on his taxes.

I used to spend some of my weekends with her when I was doing my Swiss military service. She would come pick me up at the Bülach barracks with her car, a Ford Capri which had seen better days and looked a bit like a sports car (which almost killed her—or vice versa as Anni and the Capri crashed into a post at the side of the road. Anni was disfigured, her jaw shattered, one of her cheek caved in, scars everywhere till the end of her life . . .). At times I slept seventeen hours straight during these weekends on leave. It was the healthy tiredness of outdoor exercise. She fed me smoked salmon, Gala cheese (my favorite), pickles—everything I liked. Anni would brush the uniform I hated and ironed my Zurich-colored military mousy colored shirt.

Some friends tried to get her to go back to live in Hungary. She knew people and had family there. Hungarian was her language, the only one she could speak faultlessly and without accent. Hungary was her country. With her pension in Swiss francs she could have lived there like a princess. She always refused.

During one of her visits to Budapest around 1980, those famous visits with the imitation crocodile suitcases, her gifts, her out-of-style but still Western elegance from the fifties, Anni had a new accident: she was run over by a bicycle in a pedestrian walkway. Again, there was a hospital stay, new disfiguration, new scars (repeating the repeating of her father's accident with the army truck), an endless trial, no witnesses, fake witnesses, a reluctant insurance company (it was a Swiss insurance company, the best in the world as long as all you do is sign up), it's my cousin Évi who was supposed to inherit the sum she was going to get.

But Évi also died soon after of cancer.

In this story, everyone is mortal.

(My mother had a theory about her sister: she must have led a double life. My mother at times lamented Anni's miserable, poor and solitary life and was sorry for her. She reproached me for no helping her, for not supporting her. But at other times she was angry at Anni for her far flung travels on luxurious ships—and she had lovers! The day when K. and I couldn't stay at Anni's in Seebach but had to go to the hotel, "Ádám, can you imagine! Anni must have been entertaining a man!" For my mother who loved company, society, excitement, stories, gossip, laughter, the fullness of life, it was unthinkable that an intellectual woman, a European—with all the meaning that word carried in twentieth century Hungary, in the sense Thomas Mann and Stefan Zweig gave to it—a cultured humanist, enemy of barbarism, of obscurantism and moreover her sister, had buried herself in Seebach, the dullest suburb of a gloomy city of a boring country, so as, for long years, take photos of her solitude: pictures of a quasi-moonlike, empty suburban landscape.)

# 10

## Anyu

In Hungarian *anyu* is a diminutive of *anya*, which means, you guessed it, mother. Also, and one can say: *anyuka*, little mom, or *anyukám*, my little mom—words I spoke often. There are yet other diminutives I've never used, such as *anyuci* and the triple diminutive *anyucika*, still meaning little mom, or *anyus*, reserved, in my family, for mother-in-laws (*Bíró anyus, Luy anyus*) or again *mama* or *mami* or even *mutter*, which, being of German origin, were slang. The French language, less inventive (so much less . . . but, oh, what an unwelcome comment by a Hungarian, nationalist-chauvin-

ist poorly-assimilated-undeserving-of-living-in-a-country-like-France), the French language, I'm saying, has always limited itself to *maman*, even though *maminouche, maminou, mamichou,* or *maminette* were within the grasp of all French-speaking mouths.

My mother's official given name was Georgina and more rarely on some documents, Györgyi. My daughters, my wife, and before them my French relatives called her Georgette. Her parents, Blanka and Georges (György), had wanted a boy, a György Junior (which is fairly surprising in a Jewish family where the father's name is not given to the son, but anything was possible with this grandfather Luy). But they had a girl, a Georgette . . .

Doktor Bíró Imréné (Mrs. Doctor Imre Bíró) born Luy Georgina had an unusual personality.

If I were asked to define her in one word, to reduce some-one so complex, so manifold and so irreducible, I would say: overwhelming. Not physically so, because, though she wasn't skinny, my mother has always been very beautiful. But there wasn't enough air for others to breathe around her. Her will, her demands, her presence, her words, filled the whole of the space and left no room, not a blade of grass, not a breath of air for anyone else.

When I was still a kid in Budapest she would ask me for a great number of useless things, and she continued this by letter when I was already abroad. This irritated me and I didn't always respond to her demands. But, oftentimes, I also ignored her legitimate and useful requests. Now she is dead and I am in pain because of both omissions.

She was totally altruistic, totally devoid of the tiniest bit of selfishness, and this to the point of caricature. There are thousands of ways to be present in the world, to occupy a place, to feed and sustain one's ego. This could be done through stinginess, through possessiveness, through the hunt for honors, through sacrifice, through the feeling of superiority stemming from book knowledge . . . My mother's ego fed from her will to power, to action: to be present, needed, indispensable (could it be: to be loved? I think yes). She only existed through and for others; this was her pleasure; a pleasure just as worthy as any other one. I would even say it was worth more than all the others. She was ready to be helpful to everyone, unsparing of her time, strength, energy, and even her money (she never had lots of it as my parents were always penniless, they lived only on their salaries that, as you can well imagine, didn't amount to much in the communist era).

*One day, I was greatly impressed by the gesture of one of my friends, a gesture that right away reminded me of my mother and that I would like to tell here. This friend, René, was a bookseller in Paris. He was the most generous, the funniest, the most unpredictable, and the most creative of booksellers. He wrote poems and created surrealist objects; he had given me a mirror with the inscription: "the most dangerous animal in creation." One morning, around eleven o'clock, he called me on the phone: "Where are you eating lunch?" I had no plans. He invited me to an excellent and very expensive restaurant. When I asked him what was the reason for the invitation, he answered that there wasn't any. I didn't believe him. Things are not done that way in Paris. Things are not done that way in our profession. Human relationships are not that way. Or, in other and simple words: I am not that way. René also invited one of our common friends. During lunch we ate a lot of very fine food, drank a lot of exceptionally fine wines—I remember a Château-Latour—laughed a lot. I was waiting impatiently for René to finally ask me what he wanted to ask me; to tell me why I deserved such fine fare in the middle of the week. But we were already drinking coffee and after-coffee liqueurs, and nothing was forthcoming. "Come on René, would you please tell us what's going on." "Well, I did some great business this morning so I'm flush, and I felt like inviting some friends to lunch, that's all."*

She loved me, her only son, loved me enormously, and she showed it too much, much too much. She had wanted many children—my father hadn't wanted any. I think I'm the result of a compromise—my mother, in her old age, told me she had aborted another child, before me. I assume that she did it under my father's psychological pressure, but he was not able (or did not dare?) to obtain (or demand) this sacrifice a second time.

*I often think, especially now that I'm orphaned, about the way my life would have been organized if I had had a brother (I cannot even imagine a sister; a sister is inconceivable for me. My relations with women—frantic and permanent seduction, and incomprehension and fear and desire, render this very thought impossible.) If I had had a brother, it would have been a catastrophe for him and for me. My*

*mother's concern with not favoring one or the other would have none-*
*theless led her to have a favorite, which would have caused indescrib-*
*able dramas, neuroses and tutti quanti, in the best of case ending on*
*Uncle Sigmund's or Uncle Jacques's couch,[1] or even . . . I'm afraid to*
*even think about it. And yet, now, I would very much like to have a*
*brother, an alter ego, a confident, a true friend, who would understand*
*what I am saying and thinking, what I remember and what I have for-*
*gotten-repressed. And vice versa.*

My mother loved me—and smothered me. She didn't adore
me for my real or imaginary qualities, but simply as a mother can adore a son, even one that might be mentally or physically challenged: she adored me because I was her son.

*In 1956, when I was fifteen years old, driven by what was in the air, by*
*the crushing of the Hungarian revolution, and by the other two hun-*
*dred and fifty thousand escapees, I left my parents and my country,*
*and, for a long time, claimed to be a political refugee. For years, I even*
*carried appropriate papers, the blue "Nansen passport" of refugees*
*that my fellows knew so well (does it still exist?). Some time ago, I dis-*
*covered that I really was a maternal refugee. And this in spite of the*
*fact that my mother not only gave me her approval, but even helped*
*her only and adored son to leave her forever (though in truth, no one*
*thought it would be forever).*

    *When I arrived in France in 1956, the refugees belonging to my spe-*
*cies, that of the East, of the Hungarian kind—and for a few years there*
*were no other Heroes of the Struggle Against (the remainder in small*
*letters, please) communism—were welcomed with open arms and*
*billfolds. All of the state humanitarian organizations, the* MOSSAD,

---

1. Jacques Lacan. *Trans.*

the NKVD, the GPOU, the SDECE, the EDF , the GDF, the GARP, the KGB, as well as the private ones, the NOI, the ION, the OIN, the ZOB, the BIN, the NIB,[2] all were seeking to make life easier for us. We were high-class refugees, and we took refuge in high-class luxury. But who actually knows Rwandans, Bosnians, Vietnamese, Algerians, Kurds, Albanians (Afghani have not yet arrived but they are already on their way)? In what way have they earned the gratefulness of the CHRISTIAN WEST (all in capital letters, please, it's the least one can do)? They are out of luck; there are no longer refugees, only a few asylum seekers, it's more chic but it pays less, and then they are getting here forty years too late, too bad, they should have thought of it sooner. But it was also important to know to pick the right bad guy, the most satisfying one, though of course this one no longer exists—everything slips away. My daughter J., not being able, not having to seek refuge anywhere, chose a path that is more difficult: she helps others. And you'll never guess who J. began by helping: refugees. Thus, in the family, we experience everything: the theory and the practice.

But before putting myself under the protection of NATO, the UN, Radio Free Europe and of the National Railways of France, I had a choice: I could become either a piece of soft clay in the hands of an overpowerful mother, or I could become gay, or I could revolt, and this increasingly in a permanent state of fury till the bloody rupture. I chose the third way . . . Actually it's my mother who chose the third solution for me: escape.

In fact, I had chosen freedom.

2. Some of the organizations listed here are whimsical play on strictly French puns, and others are definitely not "humanitarian." The English reader will recognize some of them, and in addition there are also such organizations as the EDF (Electricity de France), which is the national electric company. As in the earlier list of acronyms, the point is the absurdity of such lists of acronyms in themselves. *Trans.*

My mother's disorderly, irrational, and disorganized life wove together, among other things, unfulfilled desires, overflowing energy and limitless self sacrifice.

She had wanted to raise many children, to have a large family: she had only one son who ended up leaving her. She had wanted to travel, to see the world and also to see more people, to play a social role, to be a hostess and to visit: she married a man who hated any outing and travel, and who was only interested in medicine. She had great aptitude for languages, and spoke several of them, among which, surprisingly, French—while a young girl, my mother studied in Lille for two semesters and stayed with Aunt Lucie, Ernest's widow. She loved France, kept up contacts with the French branch of the family, her uncle's children and grandchildren, and would have liked to live abroad, preferably in France. Yet she had linked her destiny to a man who couldn't hear, so he wasn't interested neither in foreign languages nor foreign countries, and loved only (and this passionately) Hungary. And what's more, he distrusted France and the French, those superficial, inconsistent, and immoral beings.

*As a cosmopolitan, "wandering neuropathic Israelite" without home or country, I feel an odd hereditary-like attachment to France: while visiting Chicago's Art Institute and looking at Renoir's Two Sisters (On the Terrace) which is nothing to write home about, I couldn't understand why I was suddenly moved just because I knew that the background depicted Chatou on the Seine where we had lived. And when I see Cézanne's or Pissarro's landscapes, I feel an immense nostalgia for these landscapes, these French landscapes—as if I belonged in them, in those very landscapes. It's one of the miracles of this country: it can make you believe that you are at home. In my home. I love this coun-*

*try—which is mine, which I feel to be mine—but can one love a coun-
try? Isn't it always ourselves that we really love through a place, a
person?—this country that I see from the outside, as a Hungarian. One
day I was driving in an old Paris neighborhood with a famous French
photographer. It was raining and my passenger pointed out the shining paving stones. Look, Monsieur Adam, he said, I only see these paving stones since I saw Brassaï's photos. And do you know why he saw
them? Because he wasn't born here. He was Paris's best photographer
because he was seeing Paris with a foreigner's gaze, with the newness
of the outsider.*

My mother loved to putter around, to fix things herself,
improvising clumsily and amateurishly with pieces of rope
or tape. She loved nature and adventure, while her husband, even though very good with his hands, would never
touch a hammer, nail, or screwdriver, and preferred to hire
craftsmen—specialists on whom he looked down, just as he
looked down on all manual, administrative, and commercial
work, in short any occupation that wasn't intellectual. Moreover, he only liked the city and its comforts, which he called
civilization. My father's aversion to all words that stood for
nature was weird: flowers, even cut ones, animals, moun-
tains, streams, path, fields . . . It's not that he was simply indifferent, he hated it all.

I think that my father's deafness played a big role in all
those contradictions: fear of the foreign, abhorrence of the
sort of motion that might displace boundaries and demand
a commitment, desire for solitude. But my mother resented
my father for not having told her when they first got to know
each other that he was (already) poor of hearing. Apparently
this was also the reason my father gave for not having other

children: he was steeped in genetics of which he was one of Hungary's best specialists and was afraid of fathering deaf children. He started to test my hearing when I was three months old with a rattle he shook first next to my left ear and then to my right . . .

Did they love each other? They certainly did in the early days of their marriage. It was not an arranged marriage. How long did they date before getting married? Were they in love with each other, did they feel passion? They slept all their lives in separate rooms, but I found a box of condoms in the drawer of my father's night stand.

*I brought up this box to my mother and asked her for some sort of explanation because, at that age—nine or ten years old?—having no sister nor girls in my school, sex remained mysterious and incomprehensible, and mostly dirty and useless. I remember claiming to my school buddies that my parents had only made love once in their lives, just to make me.*

Did they love each other? My mother did not dare go on a vacation or a trip for fear of leaving my father without someone to take care of him (what care? She died at age eighty-three while my father, healthy as a horse, passed away when he was than ninety-five years old) and without food—but did she love him? She had little interest for my father's studies, his intellectual preoccupations, humanism, faith in progress, or Masonic ideals (I am not aware of any book she read from cover to cover; when I conjure her up in my imagination I see her laughing while stroking my hair or walking around Leányfalu, pulling out some weed, her arms full. The image of my mother reading a book is alien to me, while I only need to close my eyes to see my father in his armchair, holding up his broken nose with his left hand to breathe more easily, and holding a book in his right hand). Mrs. Bíró was resolutely left wing, Social-Democrat before the war and Communist afterwards. She empathized with the oppressed, championed the poor—my father was a bourgeois, though somewhat progressive but still a bourgeois, with faith in bourgeois values, in an intellectual elite, and a sort of contempt for the uneducated, the poor and the laboring classes in general, and a fear of proletarians in particular.

Did they love each other? Among my father's papers, I found letters dating from the 1950s in which my mother lavished on my father advice, care, kisses and more kisses, and words of love, and I miss you and when are you coming back (I suppose from a vacation?), a newly decorated apartment awaits you . . .

Once she retired (she had worked since she was nineteen in various organizations as a translator and archivist), my mother organized her life around two poles: her little cabin on the Danube some twenty five kilometers from Budapest and my father. (I call it her cabin because it was under her name, so much did my father not want it to be his because it represented everything he hated: lack of comfort, smallness, people having to be close to each other, mosquitoes—which I have to admit found him delicious, their favorite dessert—the disorder, unpredictability, and happenstance of nature, and flowers and trees requiring care. So much my father, who loved luxury and ostentatiousness, felt ashamed in front of people who earned a better living than he, owned bigger cars—my mother drove, quite badly at that, Fiats, which started out with the 500 model and never went beyond the 750—and more beautiful and bigger houses . . . ) Anyu spent the last years of her life disparaging Apu (my father), yelling at him, nagging him, writing him on bits and pieces of paper, no longer love letters but increasingly desperate words (the only thing I wish for is death, there's nothing to keep me alive), words that were increasingly negative about their relationship (living with you is no life, I wish we were both dead), increasingly mean (after I die you no longer will have a maid, no one will take care of you because you are so bad and selfish and you'll die in an institution for demented old people), increasingly extreme. I found a great number of those notes on all of my visits and also after my mother's death (my father didn't bother getting rid of them—did he even read them?). My father would hold the photograph of his dead wife to his heart, and he often called me Györgyi— but he requested that he be buried with his mother, and when one day an ambulance had to come pick up my mother who had collapsed from one of her heart attacks (it so happened that I had just gotten there, as if fate . . . ), my father asked the flabbergasted doctor: "can I go shave now?"

*I need to take a moment here to write more about the ambulance episode. I am coming from Paris for one of my regular visits. I go up to the second floor, and, to my surprise, I don't need to ring the bell because the door is open. I thus enter, suitcase in hand, and discover the following scene: my mother in her slip is lying on a stretcher, a nurse in a white coat in the process of giving her a shot, and another man in white is talking with my father. When my father sees me, he addresses me in an ordinary tone of voice as if he had just seen me ten minutes ago even though I had just come from the airport after six months of absence: Anyu had a heart attack, they're going to take her to the hospital. Then he turns toward the doctor and asks him permission to go shave. But the strangeness of the scene lies elsewhere: the doctor, a young intern, is the spitting image of my father thirty years ago. Moustache, black hair, piercing brown eyes . . . I think for a moment that I am hallucinating—all the more so in that the doctor, naturally, also looked like me, since it is well known that my own features are identical to my father's. For a split second, I think I have gone insane or that I am a spectator at a play acted out by my family.*

When my mother died, the first thing he told me was that he urgently wished to sell her cabin by the Danube.

Her unfulfilled and frustrated desires led to a phenomenal amount of energy. All the more so in that my mother possessed a rare physical and moral courage. She got me out from the war alive at the cost of ruses, lies, enormous sacrifices, resourcefulness—the military horse that had been shot in front of our apartment was immediately butchered so that I would have something to eat, the trip with me on the roof of one of the first packed train to work the land in a cooperative—always to be able to feed me . . . In November '56, when the Russians came back to Budapest after a sham retreat of ten days, there was street fighting. For the second time in twelve years, we got ready to go down to the underground shelter. When a column of Russian tanks stopped in front of our building and one of the tanks aimed its canon at our floor, we hurriedly grabbed our bags we had already packed (to which my father added his typewriter) to rush to the basement. At this precise moment the phone rang. I saw my mother calmly pick it up and say, as if it was the most ordinary of occurrence: "they are in front of the house, we are going down to the shelter, I'll call you back later."

*When my father died, I brought the typewriter back with me to Paris.*

In December of 1956, my mother accompanied us, Gabi and me, to the border village where the guide (hired by her and by my grandmother Blanka) was to meet us. We were waiting under the porch of a house when, instead of the guide, we saw a border patrol come by. My mother came out from our hiding place, approached the soldiers who were armed to the teeth and we watched her leave with them. She came back half an hour later, having gotten the soldiers to go away from the spot by asking them to accompany her to the other end of the village in quest of an imaginary relative. Her moral courage came close to being unconscious; in fact it was unconscious. My mother spoke her mind to everyone. She got into fights with the section secretary (of the Parti, of course), with all her superiors, with all the authorities, with all the neighbors . . . She was sued many times because she refused to compromise, to obey, to accept defeat when she felt she was in the right, or to recognize her wrongs.

But she didn't use her energy solely to engage in conflicts, and she didn't use it only to get food when there was none to be gotten, but also to buy, or when that was not possible, to have made for me open sandals of a very specific model while others, in this a poor and underequipped Budapest, felt lucky just to find anything to put on their feet. She used her courage and her indomitable combativeness to get back (a unique event in the annals of a Communist country) our country house that had already been nationalized and turned into a retirement home for the employees of a department of the state, and also to bring every evening after her work several net bags filled with what was needed to eat and live to my father and me, this at the cost of one hour and a half of traveling by bus and by tram (there's a photo of her smiling and loaded with packages). Her energy also made it possible for her (when this was again allowed) to obtain building permits and then even to build herself the vacation homes of all the members of the family and friends who asked her, and in addition to solve their marital or other problems, find them a doctor, an empty bed in the best hospital, Swiss medications, spare parts for their cars, tapes to learn a foreign language, foreign books impossible to find in Budapest, or the address of one organization or another . . . But my mother also helped those who were not asking for it, who did not want her help, who thought they could manage by themselves or who didn't need anything—but those latter had to watch out! My mother couldn't forgive them for not needing her.

There was a crowd at her funeral. I had to fight with the religious authorities who were managing the cemetery for them to agree my mother was to be incinerated as she had requested. Since the Shoah . . . , they say that "the others" have been burned enough for us not to add to them . . . I threatened to steal her body and to bring it elsewhere . . . then I paid up.

*In the enormous Jewish cemetery of Budapest, a cemetery of my own country but henceforth alien to me, far from the heart, it was as if I was alone. They put some white flower bouquets on the urn, a great silence fell, I wasn't thinking of anything, I was stricken, crushed, dead, me too, I was dead. Then the grave diggers put my mother on a hand cart that we followed through the endless alleys of the silent and unknown cemetery. I was walking ahead of the others, farther and farther from them. My father, lost, absent—what was he thinking about?—was hanging onto K.'s arm. The grave digger who was pushing the cart turned around to tell me: it's going to take a while, it's way at the other end. It was a hot day in July. I took off my jacket and carried it on my shoulder, I was walking as in a park, as on a walk, it was my last walk with Anyu who passionately loved walking. In silence I followed my mother, or rather what remained of her on the cart, I felt an immense peace in this garden, I knew instinctively and without needing to think that my life was going to be different, that henceforth I was all alone and I was going to have to live that way. But everything was peaceful, all of a sudden it was almost cool under the trees of the heat wave, and I stopped for a moment to wait for the others. I looked at the trees and I saw them differently but I didn't try to analyze this feeling. It is summer, I'm walking on leaves in a deserted cemetery behind . . . From now on it is she who is going to need me, it is I who will take care of her . . . take care, not of her urn, or her tomb, but of her memory on earth. What else was I thinking then? Nothing. During this long walk I ceded the place and the time to melancholy, to anxiety, to the nameless and diffuse misery that installed itself in me, comfortably, profoundly, forever. By the time Anyu's friends and family members in mourning arrived in front of the gaping hole where the urn that contained God knows what was going to be deposited, melancholy and misery were already at home; they will remain in this dwelling till the walk that will in turn take me in the hand cart to my own hole.*

*When they were all gathered around the grave, I stepped on a small mound of dirt; from my pocket I pulled a piece of paper folded in four on which I had carefully phonetically copied the old Kaddish. I had decided to say it for my mother despite her distaste for everything religious and despite her expressed wishes to avoid any Jewish or other ceremony. I read it with a voice chocked with emotions, addressing a* nonexistent God with sacred, incomprehensible words in a foreign language that was mine.

I had their names and dates engraved on the gravestones that were put on (above?) my parents, and we had just returned to the cemetery, with K. and Y. in August 2001. The weather was as lovely as it had been during my mother's funeral—sun, wind. The small stone with my mother's name had been cemented crookedly on the tombstone, I started to laugh and cry, because the stone worker's clumsiness had inadvertently immortalized my mother's nature, and this was good.

When I find myself in danger, when I'm really frightened of something, I call her. As I did on that cliff when it crumbled under my feet. As I do even now, at age sixty, even four years after her death. As I will till the very last of my days.

I'm walking in the rain, in Touraine, toward the farm that we bought there, and I'm thinking, my mother would have loved this place. We would have yelled at each other about the work that needed to be done in the house, of the trees to be cut or planted, about anything at all. I would have rejected her advice even if it had been wise and reasonable, so as not to submit to her law. I would have said that it was my house, bought with my money and you have nothing to say about it, you would have cried, asking me why I didn't love you, I wouldn't have answered, angry, hating those scenes, hating you, hating myself. You would have set out on foot to go back to Paris, I would have picked you up with my car two kilometers away, collapsed on the side of the road. I would have yelled at you, beside myself, you would have called the airline company to go back to Hungary im-me-di-at-ely, we would have eaten dinner, we would have talked about other things, we would have kissed before going to bed , and you would have asked me, a grandfather of sixty, if I had gone weewee before bedtime, I would have replied, exasperated, that no, I prefer to pee in my bed, it keeps me warm, you would have laughed and cried at the same time, in a way that I *am so familiar with, and asked me why I'm so mean to you and why I hate you, the morning you would have woken up well before me and walked, limping (diabetic and with a bad heart) all the way to the bakery three kilometers away to buy me croissants . . . God, how I miss you.*

When I was ten years old, the fashion in Hungary was golfing pants they called *bricsesz* (pronounced britchesse), a word probably of English origin, *bridges? Breeches?* I dreamt of having one of those pants because I loved the way the elastic at the knees made them puffy. My mother had one made for me (at the time, the Hungarian ready-made clothing industry was still in its infancy and it was cheaper to have something made). I was delighted with it—but when I wanted to wear them the first time to go to school, my mother forced me to pull the pants legs down to my calves thus ruining the puffiness and the stylishness, under the pretext that I had to cover my calves. This was the spot where all my colds started, that my calves were sensitive (for her, I was sensitive everywhere: my kidneys, my neck . . . In my mother's eye I was a sick child permanently convalescing who needed constant care to resist the outside temperature, food, the blows of fate—life itself. When I was seventeen she had my appendix taken out, even though it was fine. By correspondence, by twisting the arm of one of her friends, a Genevan doctor, she convinced him to lie to me. I now know that this attitude is common to all mothers in all poor countries, where they must struggle for clothes, for food, for survival). I was furious, and as soon as I got out the door, I pulled my pants legs up to my knees. But I remember the horrible scene one Sunday when all three of us were going to the restaurant on Marguerite Island. In the middle of the bridge, my mother noticed that the pant legs of my *bricsesz* were not down to the regulation low of my calves, and defying maternal authority, they exhibited the puffy freedom and elegance of a gentleman golfer. There followed a heated altercation with me sitting on the ground on the bridge, my mother forbidding me to come along to the restaurant, my father looking a bit lost, but still trying to support parental authority . . . I ended up going back home all alone, without lunch, without going to the restaurant, crying and cussing, but my pants legs proudly pulled up to just below the knees.

It was in 1967 that K. came with me for the first time to Budapest, to Sallai Imre Street.

*Before 1948 and again since 1989, that street was and is now called Tátra street. The unfortunate Sallai Imre had been a clandestine Communist and was killed in the thirties by firing squad after a mock trial under horthy. He was first imposed in and then erased from collective memory by rotten regimes—but do you know of any Hungarian regime that isn't rotten?—for which the act of naming or unnaming a street was, and always will be, solely political and in no way linked to the street name itself.*

When we got to the second floor, I opened the door that I hadn't opened for eleven years and we found ourselves face-to-face with my mother, half dressed with a shoe in her hand, welcoming us with the announcement that she was leaving forever, and that she was going to kill herself. My father, desperate, welcomed us with these words: "Ádám, Györgyi is leaving forever." K. was speechless, struck dumb. I told her that my mother was going to stay alive and that she was going to come back. Which she did half an hour later.

She, of course, had trouble accepting K. But not as much as I feared. I expected horrible scenes of jealousy, unfair tests that would be lost before they started—she contented herself to criticize her on some minor points and, years after I got married, she reproached me one day for having married such a "decorative" woman. In reality, my mother quickly took to liking K. and for good reasons (because of the person K. is) as well as for bad ones (because she isn't Jewish, and with her I finally put an end to "all that").

I didn't invite my parents to my wedding, and didn't even tell them ahead of time. I wrote them a letter the next day to announce it. I had for a long time stopped letting my mother know of my life in general and my relationships with women in particular (as for my father, he never showed any interest for the details of my life besides my studies). I had no desire to explain myself, to listen to comments that could be wrong or right or mean—I didn't want advice, commentaries, orders. I didn't want her to insert herself into my life. I hadn't become a maternal refugee to let myself be imprisoned all over again. As for girls, even though when I was still a child I had the impulse to confide in her, she very early on involuntarily dissuaded me.

One day while I was still in high school, my mother, during her only visit to Geneva, saw a girlfriend's photograph on my night stand. She looked at it and commented: she is small. That was true. "You're right, it's better to do it with small ones." I was dumbstruck. First, what did my mother know anyway? And then, from where did those scientific comments come from? "Small ones do it better..." And anyway, what business of hers was it? What right did she have... in short. The woman's question was taken care then and there, for the rest of our lives.

*There was never to be a name, an event, an allusion, not a single word.*
*(It is during that same visit that my mother wanted us both to ride on*
*my motor scooter to the Côte d'Azur...)*

I never took seriously the suicide threats and the black-mail until I found out that my mother had swallowed one (or two?) containers of extra powerful heart medication. It happened in her Leányfalu house, in the evening, and the fact that a neighbor came to borrow something and found her lying on the floor already unconscious was an accident close to a miracle. Ambulance, night in the hospital—they only told me several months later. Why this gesture? Did she really want to die, or was it a cry: "Love me! I want to be loved, I give so much to others, give my something back, your love!"

The last time I saw her was in the hospital, in a sordid ward shared by eight dying women. She had just had a heart attack—yet another one—and I came urgently from Paris, but she was already getting ready to get out the next day (which she did against her doctors' advice). A silver plane was crossing a clear sky; my mother looked at it for a long time with tears in her eyes. Ever since, every time I see a plane-bird-trip-freedom-liberation-escape-dream-desire illuminated by the sun, I think of my mother, of the last image I have of her. Then a few days later, a phone call to Paris . . . Someone mercifully closes the door to my office.

She died during the night; I found the last sentence she wrote to my father before going to bed: "Tomorrow I must get up early to go to the doctor." She certainly must have called out to her deaf husband sleeping at the other end of the apartment . . . or to her son, one thousand and six hundred kilometers away . . .

My mother made me take English lessons, which was not without risk in this country occupied and dominated by the Soviet Union where the study of Russian was required in all grades, and where all the English teachers had to recycle themselves into Russian ones.

She also made me learn music. The violin? The piano? The flute? You still don't know my mother. It was the ukulele.

# 11

## Apu

When my father became too old to still function in his job, the management of the Sports Hospital of the Hungarian state, where he was director of the ophthalmology department, asked him to retire. He refused immediately, instinctively, as if he had been politely and nicely asked to lie down in his grave while still alive and keep quiet. So then, could you please come less often, get some rest, but I'm not tired, you could give us advice, be our consultant—he did understand, but he clung to the idea of being able to still go to the hospital. He wrote me, "can you imagine, I'll only go to the

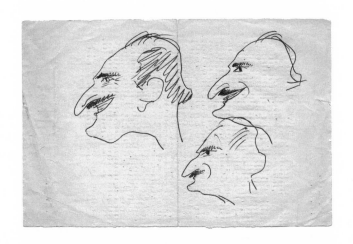

140

hospital two or three times a week, what am I going to do with my time, the rest of the week, the rest of my life, what is going to happen to me? I, who has never done anything else other than medicine, than work! What?"

I always thought my father had a beautiful style, a real writing talent, even when writing simple letters. His style was a bit grandiloquent, a bit pompous, a bit theatrical (theatrical as he himself was: the style is the man), a bit out-dated, but perfect and noble, with well-balanced sentences with his own personal rhythm, a well-chosen and very broad vocabulary, and never a mistake. As a young man, he was writing for his uncle's paper, the *Nagyvárad*. Later on he translated Goethe, and later on again, when he was already old, he wrote two short stories about a youthful love. After high school he had wanted to be a journalist, a writer. I think it is his father who forced him to become a doctor, he who was frightened of blood his whole life long. (He had a col-league come to give my mother a shot.) My grandfather was supposed to have told him: on the other side of the border, a Hungarian author is not even a street sweeper. But my grandfather couldn't have foreseen that his son was going to venture so little on the other side of the border. And yet, it must also be said that medicine saved my father's life during the war. To come back to less distant times, I thus advised my father to write his autobiography. "You passed through a whole century," "but, you know, it's really the century that passed through me, look in what state it has left me, they don't even want me anymore." He had a sense of humor that was refined and sharp; he told his stories the way he gave his lectures—they were remarkably constructed; he cultivated the suspense, the endings. He loved jokes and word play

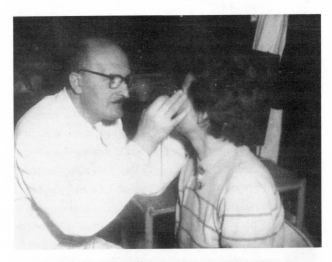

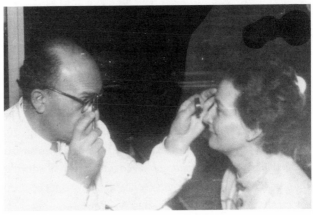

(though less than Grandfather Luy). Even though he was not talkative, even a bit taciturn, my father was the star at social events where, in spite of his poor hearing, he shined, he was the center. He told stories, anecdotes. He made people laugh so he wouldn't be forced to listen to them. They were dazzled, dazzled by my father, by his sense of culture. Often when he was still young, once his act was over, he would get up and order my mother to follow him. Later on, his impatience did not lessen but, as his deafness became total, he no longer dared leave these social gatherings lest he should attract attention to his disability.

When I think, when I was thinking, saying, writing that all the political parties and unions are fighting to get the retirement age lowered, and even my friends, around me, even though much younger than I, and you . . .

*And now that I am sixty years old and my friends are obviously just as old, I see them leaving—what am I saying—rushing toward retirement, to retirement, into retirement . . . Work is evil.*

Yes, "and I," answered my father, "doctor and only doctor, I want to remain doctor, and I don't want to retire from anything, neither from work, nor from life, which is the same thing. I will write, you're right, I have seen and experienced so much." One day, about six months later, I got a letter: "I finished my autobiography, it was your idea, I thank you, it occupied and entertained me, I had to do lots of research, and relive my memories, it was at times painful," writes my father, "I am retyping it and I'll send it to you." The mailman brought me a fairly fat envelope containing thirty two typewritten pages. Is that all? That's his autobiography? Seventy years of life? And the text: names of doctors, dates, addresses of hospitals in Hungary, clinics, sanatoriums, their directors, the assistants, the patients, the illnesses, the discoveries, the financial difficulties of the hospital, the professional difficulties of the doctors. About the births, the fate, the deaths of the members of his family: nothing. Love, childhood and juvenile loves, women: zero. My mother: the date of their marriage. Trips: what trips? World War I: three lines; the Republic of the Soviets of Kun Béla, in 1919: two lines; World War II: what war? Where? Forced labor in the disciplinary regiment, the killing of a part of his family: two lines; his native town, his childhood, the semi-fascist regime of admiral horthy, Communism, Russian occupation: each time one or two lines; his health, his deafness, his political ideas, his conception of the world, the Freemasons, philosophy, religion, Judaism, God: nothing—silence. Thirty two pages of doctors, of unknown-forgotten names, of dead MDs, of hospitals whose staff, names and even the streets where they were located have dropped into the void . . . However: long passages on education, on schools, primary, secondary, on the teachers, their names, listed by their disciplines, on the university . . . on studies.

"But Apu, and your life? The things you saw? Wars, revolutions, and the rest? You have made a few . . ."

"Listen Ádám, nobody is waiting for me to tell about World War II. Others have already done it, much better than I could. The same goes for Kun Béla . . .

"But you, where are you in all this?" (I must say that my father hated to talk about himself. The reason I know nothing about, for instance, his childhood or even his teen years, is because he was secretive rather than modest, and he did not give anything away.)

"I am a doctor. Who still knows the name of the director of the number two ophthalmology clinic in 1948? And who still remembers the name Schulek, who was the teacher of my own teacher, Professor Grósz Emil? And last-minute complications during some major surgeries? Who will tell you about them? Thirty-two pages, Sonny (he often called me this), it's my life in great detail. You know what I did on this earth? Medicine. With the people whose names you can find in these thirty-two pages. I practiced medicine in hospitals by taking care of patients and saving their lives. This is what I need to tell. You suggested I write my autobiography. So what is it, an autobiography? It's the story of a life by the one who lived it. So here it is, my life. My work. Now I would like to find a publisher for it."

To find a publisher, what a joke . . . for thirty two pages! Written by someone known for his brilliant style, his humor but, here, these pages so boring . . . devoted to work, only to work.

*And yet . . . now, as I am evoking my father's memory, this tireless worker, I remember Vermeer's* Milkmaid, *a painting I saw in Amsterdam. What struck me in this painting so much more that the obvious pictorial mastery, it's the subject: the total attention that the woman devotes to her duty. She is performing a humble task—it's barely work. But she is there, completely there, and we have to say, dare to say because it is unmistakable, it is from that very gesture of pouring milk from a pitcher into a dish that her peace, her happiness, her total happiness comes from. There is no work more human than this, more useful, nobler. I've rarely seen someone work this way; this milkmaid shines with peace and letting go of the self. I would like to be like her. Like she is, and not like the French painter who said that he threw himself into his work as if he wanted to kill somebody. No, like her: to consent, to accept, to love. There, yes, work has meaning. It is no longer work. It's life itself, stripped, it's being. Holland was at war at that time; people were dying—this woman perhaps did not even know*

*it; nothing seems to exist for her outside of her work; and it had to be*
*so for the war to have meaning . . . (does it ever? . . . so rather, lets just*
*say it had to be for a victory, any victory, to be useful for something).*
*That woman had to, she must, be able to pour milk, for all eternity, by*
*lifting the pitcher with both her hands.*

What if this was my father's secret? Or what if, on the
contrary, his attachment to work was only an escape? Or indifference?

Six months before his death, I understood that my father
had given up, that he was going to die. A friend asked me to
give him an article about his teacher who had taught him to
think and to live (my father, in contrast to my mother and
myself, bestowed admiration easily and widely: Leonardo da
Vinci, Robespierre, Napoleon, Goethe, Helmholtz, Kossuth,
the leader of the 1848 revolution—but above all the subject
of the article in question: Professor Grósz Emil whom I just
mentioned, one of the founders of Hungarian ophthalmology, and moreover a compatriot, an one also native of Nagyvárad. My father idolized him: he learned his profession at
his side, he was one of his assistants, he referred to him as
"my teacher," his son was his best friend . . . Later on, he even
devoted to him the only book he wrote for the nonscientific
general public, *A Clinic Must Not Die*—a best seller that went
out of print and then was reprinted . . . ). My father was lying down, did not want to get up, said he was tired. He had
stopped reading, stopped watching TV. I triumphantly
handed him the newspaper. He very carefully and slowly
put on his glasses, looked at the time, then read the title of
the article, which in earlier times would have excited him:
"Homage to Grósz Emil" . . . He took off his glasses carefully,

gave the paper back to me and said in a completely indifferent tone of voice: "Grósz Emil," then he turned over toward the wall.

I understood then that it was the end. I didn't know when it would happen. He was a tree, a force of nature. I wished for his death, because I thought his life had lost all meaning, its reason for being—but I was lost. I was thinking at the same time that the meaning of life was in life itself, sleeping, breathing, seeing, and that would be enough. It is not right to kill the mentally disabled—I'm viscerally against euthanasia. I'm in agreement with Camus on this—life, nothing but life. We do not kill old people with dementia. And yet . . . the life of this brilliant man, crushed, lying there, sleeping all the time, seemed to me so empty . . . Was he suffering? My love and respect for this father of mine was boundless—you surely can see that. But I loved him more than myself, and I did not want to wish that he would live in a vegetative state just for me. In fact, he was conscious but tired. Of what? I was sitting by his bedside. Suddenly: "Say Ádám, do you think I'm going to die?"—he asked me in a neutral and informative tone as if he was asking me what time it was. I replied that there was no hurry. "Oh, alright," he answered in a tone of voice that was a bit annoyed—perhaps disappointed.

Sometimes on Sundays we used to go to the restaurant—what a treat! My mother of course was a fine cook, but, like all the women in Hungary at the time she had to make do with a shortage of ingredients: no meat, no this, no that. Restaurants, rather, certain chic restaurants (that is if one can say "chic" about anything in Hungary during those years) such as the Grand Hotel of Marguerite Island had meat on Sundays.

Thus one Sunday, all three of us were on our way to that

restaurant on the island. The maitre d' was extremely, excessively, obsequious. This way, Professor, Sir, take this table you'll be protected from the spring sun, which has come early and which is already, oh yes, very hot (we were eating in the garden even though my father hated the outdoors). I will be the one who'll take care of you, Professor, is this your son Professor—he's so tall, and he wipes the chair, and cleans the tablecloth yet again, and holds the chair while the professor sits down, and he calls the professor's wife, "your lady highness."[1] I thought this was so weird and he kept it up all the way through the meal. The meal over, we went back on foot, the way we had come, through the island and then across Marguerite bridge. I asked my father from where he knew this maitre d'—because it was obvious they knew each other. He responded with a vague gesture, a bit evasive, mumbled some inaudible words, while turning his head away. Then he went on, happy and enthusiastic on the beauty of the river, its breath which still surprised him, and the extraordinary view from this particular bridge, and his standard spiel, the splendor of Budapest, etc. Contrary to my usual cheeky boyhood habits, I did not insist and my mother didn't say anything.

One day, months later, I was spending the afternoon seated on the ground absently and with little enthusiasm arranging in an album stamps of the two headed empire that Grandfather Luy had just given me. My father was reading, engrossed in a book.

1. This is the literal translation of the Hungarian *Nagyságos asszony*, a form of address that might have been originally used for the nobility but that became a way subalterns would address a bourgeois woman—as for instance a maid addressing her mistress. *Trans.*

"Apu, who was the maitre d' on the island when we went to eat there with you and *anyu?*"

"Oh, no one really. He was part of the cadres of my disciplinary company."

My father had replied in the most ordinary of tone while continuing to read.

I didn't know then the sinister, horrible meaning of the word "cadres" (*keretlegény*): they were the ones who would execute with a bullet in the neck workers (in fact detainees) too slow or sick during forced marches, who tortured them, who had life and death power over them.

"What disciplinary company?"

The one in which he served during the war. In a mine, at Recsk or Mátraderecske. In fact the whole of the company was sent to the Russian front. Few members of these units came back from the front: those who did not die of the cold, exhaustion, or typhoid fever were sent to the front line, to clear mines, cut barbed wires . . . those on the opposite side, the Russians, would shoot them down like rabbits. Doctor Bíró got to remain in Hungary, saved by medicine: they needed him. The cadres had no doctor. Yet he had to labor at all tasks in the mine, underground, like the others, but he had the right to wear gloves to keep his fingers more or less intact in case of need.

"Was he a nazi, A fascist? An arrow-cross?"
I was ten years old.

"Hm, I don't know. Perhaps just a poor peasants' son, he wasn't the meanest there."

It was as if I was hit by . . . no, it was . . . you can't feel what I felt. With everything I had heard at home, at school . . . I had not seen any nazi since the end of the war, I thought they had all disappeared, that they had evaporated and that the country was now only inhabited by men who were pure, brave, with transparent and irreproachable pasts.

"Apu, didn't you turn him over to the police?"

He put down his book for a moment, looked at me very calmly, with his very innocent great big brown eyes. "No, I did not turn him in to the police, what's the use? The war is over, it's too late; the dead cannot be brought back to life."

We had no discussion of crime and punishment, on the prevention of evil, we did not speak of it anymore, I asked no other questions, on collective responsibility and individual culpability, on the exemplary nature of punishment, on its usefulness, on opportunism, on cowardice . . . I told you I was ten years old, my father around fifty . . . And now that I am much older than he was then, do I know? Though at that age, I did know. The guilty had to be punished. Simple as that. That's the way it was done in school, and at home too.

My father kept on reading in silence, I pretended to be interested by the stamps . . .

("Your father was a coward."

"No, he was not."

"Then he was like Camus's stranger. Indifferent, or worse, he quit."

"From what? Since he never belonged to anything?! He survived in immobility. Like a tree. Like shellfish. So there's the rub. He was outside of almost everything. So from what could he have quit?"

"Your Doctor Bíró, how could he have believed in medicine? In healing the sick?"

"Good question. I don't know. But he did believe in it. Perhaps he loved human beings . . . the quality of humanness . . .")

On a school vacation day I accompanied my father to his hospital. Young boy that I was (very young, but what age? I can't remember) I wanted to see the building where my mother, always ill, had gone so often, of which the whole family spoke with a respect mixed with fear, with deference, and of which the head, the king, the general, the president, appeared to be my father. We had taken the tram. My father took this route every day, knew it by heart, by head, by sensing, by all his senses. At the stop, a sign warned that there was work being done on the rails, and that the stop had been moved by 200 meters. My father, who had not seen the sign, not looked at it, seeing the route unfold in his mind, the boring but vital ribbon of the path that had been inscribed, interiorized, so long ago, suddenly became very worried. What's happening? He first asked me, then the other passengers. Everyone calmed him down. The other people had paid more attention, they were less familiar with the route. But my father did not believe them. This had never happened to him, in all the years he used this line. The tram was never going to stop, never; it was going to continue its tortuous path that inexorably was to lead first to the edge of madness, and then to death itself. Then the tram slowed down and stopped. We could see the hospital, and even the usual tram stop, where several workers in blue overalls were busy. Apu, once his feet were again on solid ground after getting off the tram, quickly and strongly grabbed my hand. He was shaky and upset and whispered to me:

"I have never had such an adventurous journey."

As I said, I was very young, but I remember this trip better than other ones, longer and more futile.

He was a giant in strength, physical equilibrium and

health. I have to say that he did all he could to take care of himself. Well before there was talk of cholesterol, he avoided eating fatty food; and anyway he ate little, slowly, chewing deliberately, favoring fruits, never pork, which he found too fat, too strong in taste—he didn't like strong tastes, hated onions, peppers, spices. The only thing he really liked were cakes—and these immoderately. Cream cakes, chocolate cakes . . . till his last days when he was only eating sweets. And with all that, not the slightest trace of diabetes or excess of triglycerides. Never any alcohol, never any tobacco, never in all his life. He deeply despised drinkers and smokers, along with card players and other gamblers. Just as he despised the young people who went out in the evening to enjoy themselves, and even, *horribile dictu,* to dance. Moreover, he led a very disciplined life: in bed by ten (with his trousers carefully folded under the mattress) and up by seven. In his youth, he played tennis and went swimming, and then kept on swimming till the end. I have a photo of him at the pool when he was twenty-three years old: handsome, posing with all of his muscles flexed, a true athlete, a body builder.

It was very hard for me to watch his physical decline in his last year. This powerful man who had always held himself straight as a poplar, without an ounce of fat, muscular, his stomach flat, with a military bearing, next to whom I looked like an old man with my back bent, my drooping shoulders, and my stomach jutting forward, he had become a weak old man walking with difficulty, needing help getting on and off sidewalks, needing help to wash in the shower, and even worse. I have to say, though, that he was by that time near ninety-five and that in the summer of 1999 (he was born in 1905) the two of us along with K., had gone to swim at the pool on Marguerite Island . . . but this isn't important. In my eyes, he was a colossus, and it was incomprehensible to see him in the hands of a nurse at any age.

I have given a lot of thoughts to the reasons for his longevity.

First of all, he enjoyed exceptional physical fitness. This is the scientific aspect, genetic or accidental.

Then he had healthy life habits along with perfect self control, an iron discipline.

And yet seldom was the saying "There's no one more deaf than he who doesn't want to hear" more true. In order to live and to survive, to be able to live in peace, he closed his ears—he closed himself to my mother to begin with, to her commands and countercommands, recriminations and complaints, and her torrent of words. He then closed himself to the times, the twentieth century and its horrors that touched him directly: the extermination of a part of his family, father, brother, cousins, uncles, aunts . . . And considering he was a Hungarian in Romania, a died-in-the-wool pacifist in two wars and two revolutions, a Jew under horthy and hitler, an anti-Communist Freemason under rákosi and stalin . . . What could be worse? In a hostile and troubled context and environment, he chose peace and silence. Absence.

He had an unusual ability to avoid being concerned: neither by the times, nor by family, or by people; no problem ever disturbed his sleep—which was legendary. He was as impervious to worries and anxiety as he was to physical ailments.

And then, he died in the hospital after two (two!) surgeries under total anesthesia in the space of ten days.

*His thigh bone was broken in two places and was horribly operated on.*
*The pins came out of the bone in a scandalously bad hospital; I have to*
*write its name here: Árpád Hospital in Ujpest. Perhaps a Hungarian*
*Minister of Health will read these lines—if he knows how to read that*
*is—and will close this dilapidated building along with its incompe-*
*tent doctors.*

A doctor I knew, one of my cousins, the only good one in
that hospital, told me that a fifty-year-old man could envy
my father's heart. The same for his digestive system, his
liver, his lungs, and the rest. The fact that my father avoided
being concerned in general naturally also implied a good
amount of selfishness. In contrast to my mother who was interested in everyone except herself, my father found no one
interesting. He was tried to block out and avoid pain (his
own and that of others) as well as great passions. The only
passions (pretty weak ones at that) that I knew him to have
were for sweets, medicine, the genetics of the eye (he gave
his name to the Bíró syndrome, an abnormal and hereditary
crossing of the veins at the back of the eye), the necessity to
please, and reading . . . and repetition. He liked to go always
to the same place, he loved punctuality and regularity. He
loved habits. Even when close to senility, the nurse had to
accompany him to the same pastry shop at the same time
everyday and he always ate the same piece of cake. One of his
many slogans was: "never stray from the known path into
the unknown," a slogan that made me so angry I was beside
myself, particularly coming as it did from a scientist. This
hatred, this mistrust of anything new . . . My father was a
man of the nineteenth century: he didn't talk on the phone,
refused to buy a hearing aid for the longest time and when

my mother finally forced him to buy one, he refused to adjust it to his ear, so that in fact he wasn't using it; he didn't know how to drive and didn't want to, he refused my present of a fax machine to enable him to communicate with me once he lived alone. As for electronic gadgets, be it simple calculators or computers and all the rest, let's not even talk about it . . . I am wondering if he even noticed they existed. I still have the bittersweet memory of my embarrassment as we waited in line at a bank and my father, this man with a superior intelligence, cultivated, and particularly brilliant in math, refused to understand the function of the panel with lit numbers indicating that the teller was ready for the next customer who had taken a number from the dispenser.

During my childhood, he displayed an almost compulsive modesty (and so did my mother, I have never seen my parents naked). He never cussed, never used a dirty word, never the slightest allusion to sex, or bodily functions, to urine, or fecal matter. As to women, the topic was totally taboo. When I was around thirteen fourteen years, I dreamt about women (even when young, I was and I remain burdened with heterosexuality), I was crazy about them, they were inhabiting almost all of my cells (in my body and my brain)—but with my father, there was never a single word, not even the vaguest of hint . . . I knew that he liked being seductive, posturing, playing the peacock, displaying his wit in front of the ladies, I saw him court beautiful women in a style that was a bit excessive, out of date and ridiculous—or that I thought was ridiculous, but I noticed that women loved the clicking of heels together and the hand kissing, and that they didn't at all find exaggerated compliments outdated, on the contrary . . . Later, I discovered he loved women and they returned the sentiment. After my mother's death, I went to see him in Budapest every two or three months. We ate, of course, in the same restaurant where he always ate the same thing. He had always been extremely impatient and it had gotten worse with old age.

*I resemble him in this. I feel it, I try to fight it, but my lack of patience is stronger than me; it's a powerful internal physical need.*

We enter the restaurant when, even before taking off his coat, he starts to yell (he was already completely deaf), to demand the menu and mineral water, and then, as soon as he sits down and without waiting for me, he orders his food, while harassing the young and very pretty waitress. I feel very uncomfortable, I write in the notebook I always carried with me: "take it easy, we are not the only customers, she has to wait on other tables," but my father ignores me, keeps on yelling, demanding, complaining about the slowness of the service. I write him that we are going to be kicked out if he keeps up this circus. Suddenly, as the young woman passes by our table, my father grabs her bare arm, caresses it and tells her, you are so pretty, I (he says "I" not "we") am lucky to be waited on by you. The meal continues in this manner. The last bit of coffee barely swallowed, my father, still yelling, demands the check, which can't arrive fast enough for him . . . When the waitress brings it, I apologize very embarrassed for my father's behavior. She gives me a puzzled look and caresses (yes!) my father's head and says with a charming smile: your daddy is so nice.

What was his secret?

A few months after his death, I went back to his pastry

shop. I bought his favorite piece of cake, and paid with a very large bill, and I told the employee, a stunning redhead, to keep the change. It was much more than change, the ratio was about one hundred to five. She didn't understand. "It's to make up for all the tips my father didn't give you during all the years he came here to drink his hot chocolate and eat his cake." "Is your father Professor Bíró? We haven't seen him for months." I told her that Professor Bíró would no longer come because he was dead. She didn't know . . . and she started to cry. She, this sexy young woman, cried her heart out when she heard that this occasional customer, a grumpy ninety-five-year old man, was dead. She categorically refused the tip; I had to insist, to ask her to keep it in memory of my father—what else could I give?

My father's relationship with money, which he always hated (or was indifferent to?) became even odder after my mother's death. Since his salary from the Hungarian Institute of Oncology, for which he was still a consultant until one year before his death, and his pensions from the sports hospital and from the Academy were always deposited directly into his account, and all of his bills were automatically paid from it, my father lost contact with money. Or did he decide to stop understanding it, since my mother always took care of their finances? He, who was so generous, even prodigal, gave one penny tips; when he gave money to the nurse to do the shopping for the week he gave her the equivalent of one dollar. Or was that a ruse? When the nurse I had hired had to be paid for the first time, I came from Paris and asked my father for money knowing that he had enough in his bank account to pay a portion of this regularly. He looked at me, surprised and angry, and said, "don't you dare pay her. She takes care of me out of love." I thus had to pay her secretly, without my father knowing.

In fact he was indifferent to money all his life. It was my mother who dealt with both their salaries, she was the one who did all the shopping (for bread, milk, house, apartment, car) and who took care of their joint bank account—when at the close of the Communist era banking activity started up again and people did open bank accounts.

And yet . . . I discovered that at the end of his life, during at least his last two years, my father played lotto with passion and religiously would watch the weekly drawing on the TV. (Passion and religion were neither part of his life, nor his vocabulary.) What would this old man do with money, he who no longer spent anything, no longer bought clothes, hated travel all of his life—he who didn't need anything, who no longer aspired for anything, particularly possessions.

While he was indifferent to money, he despised business. Why? Was it to show that the stereotype of Jews and money was wrong? Was it because he truly felt money to be alien to him? During one of my visits to my parents (visits that I hated because each time I saw them getting a bit older, which gave me pain and brought me closer to their death—and to mine), my father asked me to go with him to the Academy library where, as an academician, he had the right to read and work. The Oncology Institute had requested him, at age ninety(!), to write the history of cancer research in Hungary. He took a lot of notes, read a lot—and then slowly, his head worked less and less well, and I caught him, in the Academy library, doing crossword puzzles in the newspapers put at the disposal of the learned readers. In the course of my visit with him to the library, he introduced me to the coat-check lady, whom he had known for thirty years. "This is my son, a researcher in Paris." I didn't protest, but when we got home, I asked him: "why did you say I'm a researcher when you know full well that I'm a publisher?" My father gave me one of his angry looks and answered: "you don't think I was actually going to tell her that you're a merchant in Paris?!" "Daddy, what are you talking about?" "You sell books." (The irony of fate was realized some years later, a few weeks before his death, when he no longer wanted to get out of bed, when he pretended to read but he was no longer reading, when he was increasingly losing his sense of reality and confused names, people, day, night and hours, that he took me for his brother more and more often, even telling me one day: "you and me, we are orphans," he asked me: "what is my profession?" "Apu, you are a retired doctor." "Oh! I thought I was a publisher." "No, Apu, it's I who is a publisher, in Paris. You, you are a doctor." "That's true, Ádám is a publisher in Paris.")

He was intolerant and impatient. The proof? Here are two instances. He failed a man on his eye exam though the man had perfect vision. He wanted to become pilot for Malév airlines but he was uneducated. Even though his name was Arany János (one of the great Hungarian poets of the nineteenth century), he was ignorant of the very existence of his famous namesake. The equivalent in France in 1987 would be for a Monsieur Victor Hugo to have never heard of the other Victor Hugo. Another example among many: he once noticed three customers at a table in the patio of a restaurant eating dinner at four o'clock in the afternoon. He gave them a stern lecture: "Aren't you ashamed? Eating dinner at four o'clock?" Order had to rule, and the one who moved boundaries, who opened the door to motion, should beware.

During his lifetime, I was not aware of any extramarital affairs, but I thought that with time, someone would talk and I might learn a thing or two. The silence surprised me all the more because right after my mother's death, my father at the age of eighty-two indulged in a senile sexuality that, in my opinion, revealed his past and/or desires that had been carefully hidden or buried. So, when we were walking in the street, he would address young women from a distance: "you have beautiful legs" (you can well imagine, how I . . . ). When following my mother's coffin, he called someone's attention to his housekeeper's legs (this person told me later). Likewise, in the tram, he would comment very loud on mini-skirts, knees, and legs. I was embarrassed, surprised and at the same time worried. If he kept this up or went further, someone was going to complain and he would be institutionalized. But I had promised him that I would never let him be put in a retirement home and that he would die at home. The first nurse I found for him in a hurry (it was urgent, he had fallen in the bus, and had hurt his back and wasn't able to get up) was a nineteen-year-old young woman (whom we found out later was also a thief). In my presence, my father, this paragon of modesty and virtue asked her, "Would you like to lie down behind me?"

The only suspicious trace of a passage to action by this unabashed Don Juan was a photograph in which my father wearing his white doctor's coat, thus at the hospital, is seated on a low wall in the sun next to a very beautiful young woman with a large bust. He is looking at the camera and is jovial, very relaxed, without the theatrical "photo-pose" that I am so used to see him take. She has a modest smile, and on the back of the photograph in my father's handwriting there's the name of the young woman, a doctor, and "1955, after the sweater." Feel free to interpret this anyway you want.

Though it pained me to witness his physical deterioration (a late and brief one) I suffered much more when faced with his senility, which, as I only now realize, started much earlier. The fact that he no longer recognized people, that he mistook night and day, that he depended entirely on his nurse, that the only human contact this highly literate man who read and spoke(!) Latin had was this woman who, though very nice, very helpful, was uneducated, troubled me a lot. But other things totally upset me. My father was a model of masculine elegance. He used to go back home on the way to the hospital if he noticed a missing button or a stain on his shirt. But this old man now wore jackets and shoes with holes and dirty shirts—and when I offered to buy him some shoes and a coat, he objected. After his death, I found in his closet the new shirts still in their untouched store wrappers I had given him. He ended up neglecting himself, dressing badly, indifferent to his appearance. He had become dirty— the meticulously clean doctor would now throw wrappers, all sorts of things in the street, no longer flushed the toilet, refused to take a shower—only the compulsive ceremony of a half an hour of shaving remained.

What did this letting go of self mean? Was nothing worth anything anymore? Did he give up? Was he awaiting death? I am aware that this fact of the elderly letting themselves get dirty is clinically known, studied and described. But to me, seeing it affect my father and seeing how the fall was so great and so brutal, was tragic.

I also noticed other changes in his behavior. I remember, as I am writing this, the shock I felt about ten years before his death when I noticed his love for television, for asinine programs, stupid games and silly serials such as *Derrick, Le Saint*. He had been for me the personification of pure intellect. But there was worse: he had become a liar, a prevaricator, and a boor. I already gave the example of the Academy library where he was defacing the newspapers but he was rude in the shops and refused to wait in line.

*My God, old age is truly a shipwreck. How will I be? And why am I talking so much of my father's deterioration and death? Am I that afraid?*

When I was a child, my father had been a well-known personage, a well-known scientist, and particularly a famous doctor, a "great patron." I had naively imagined that in his old age he would be surrounded by friends, respectful colleagues, and that if he ever had to be hospitalized (a thought I had blocked out as I was thinking and hoping that he would die in his sleep, at home, just as I am wishing for myself) it would be under optimal conditions: the best doctors, the best care, in a private room . . . It took me a long time to understand: my father was a survivor. In this country, Hungary, where the expected life span was sixty-five for women and sixty-three for men, none of his colleagues, none of his friends were still alive. And there was no one around who still knew him. In the miserable ward of the sinister hospital I talked about earlier, his eight fellow patients (the same number as in my mother's hospital, which was barely less sordid than his) called him sweetly but condescendingly

"Little Father Bíró." There, he was only an unknown elderly man, moreover a deaf one with whom it was no longer possible to converse, never again, just another dying patient, the least of the concerns of the young doctors who had never heard of the Bíró syndrome. It was not only no longer possible to save him but also useless. They had their hands full with younger patients at death' door—they were not about to go to extremes to prolong the life of an old man who had already lived longer than everybody else, outlasted his allotted time on earth. I had to ply the nurses with tips so that they would at least give him something to drink and clean him. I even offered an envelope to the doctor who operated (badly) on him, but he refused it.

*When I handed the money to one of the nurses, she indicated with her eyes the pocket of her blouse where I should slip the bill. Once the maneuver was delicately and discretely accomplished, she whispered to me: more. Surprised, I looked in my pocket for another bill when she added laughing: not money but do touch my breast again.*

He died there, the "great patron" who had lived for medicine, for the patients: a poorly taken care and neglected dying nobody.

As an only child, I inherited everything from my father: the apartment, his library and all of his papers. Among the mound of paper thus inherited, among the official papers I already mentioned, I discovered a wrinkled spiral bound notebook, with my father's jottings—I would recognize his beautiful handwriting, so very clear and orderly, among a thousand—with a red pencil, obviously in a hurry, without any date, all in abbreviations not always easy to decipher or guess, and of course in Hungarian. Here is my attempt at translation.

---

On the beach of Cartagena de Indias in Columbia, black and métis street sellers are offering

*massage*

*sunglasses*

*cigarettes*

*Havana cigars*

*exotic fruits (exot. for me)*

*coffee*

*Swiss watches*

*fresh water*

*mineral water*

*fruit juices*

*ice cream*

*necklaces*

*life jackets*

*collectors' coins*

*collectors' stamps (lots of Austria-H, portraits of Franz-Josef,*
*strange in the tropics)*

*purses*

*backpacks*

*leather belts*

*oysters*

*crabs*

*brightly colored shirts*

*straw hats*

*caps*

*sandals*

*shorts*
*beach dresses*
*engravings of the old town*

Also parading were
*soothsayers*
*hairdressers*
*1 music band*
*draftsmen*
*pedicures*
*manicures*

S.
had her hair done
had a massage on the ground by an enormous Negress who
drank all my bottle of Coca-Cola wtht asking,
had her fortune read in the lines o h hand (I realized: her tiny
hand; the source of immense pleasures),
called the band who played for u Columb. tunes dur. 1 hr (she
sang and danced with them),
had her finger toe nails done

I bought her
*sunglasses*
*a leather purse*
*a skirt*
*a straw hat*
she drank
*three coffees (Columb. tasteless)*
*three rhum with Coc-Col*
*guava juice (name of this fruit in Hung?)*

She ate

*fruits*

*oysters*

*crabs*

*ice cream*

she smoked

*Marlborough non stop, with her sml cig. holder in*

Full happiness. We aren't doing anything. Nothing that could be called "doing," except swimming, looking at the sea from our beach reclin. eatg, drinkg; at the hotel: fucking. All t time when we are at the hotel; we f. The skin of my prick is scratched, raw. (She shaves her sex.). I'm in pain, I put ointment on it, it gets on her nerves, I have to do it, otherwise I would be in too great pain and I couldn't f. her anymore. This idea terrifies us. I buy her plenty things, everything she asks for, she asks for ev. Nothing for me.

I look at the sea for hours. Without moving in the beach recl. Vaguely think of my life back there (never ag going to places where one can see the sea) My life: total immobility, since forvr, since birth. Worshiped work. Nothing else. Fear of what? Why no travel? Not leaving country of sleep of misery, H.? Nev joined Party? Or Orthodox Jew? Or secret opposition? Or militant Zionist? Or struggle to make lots of money? Or top athlete? Or soldier, war, Spanish Civil War? Or collector? Compulsive, paintings, engravings, books, stamps, coins, medals, match boxes, butterflies, buildings, cars, beer caps, like C.? Or rake, party animal, or heavy drinker, drug addict?

I'm looking, nothing's happening, no boat, only water, waves. Sun, a bit cloudy. The tropics. I'm looking. I'll nev see this again.

Water. I note its variations, its movts. I have seen them. I have them.

S. wants me to take phot. I refuse. "I don't have a camera." She doesn't understand. Don't you want a phot of me? Of us? Doesn't give a damn about phot of us; wants to be photographed, looked at, seen, admired, center of interest, wants to play the black star.

To remain here. To sleep at night in the ditch behind the beach, und coconut, palm trees and (don't know the names), like the others, the "secretaries" as they are called here, rent out beach chairs during the day to tourists, bring them food drink. Or not ev that. Not ev beg. Nothing. Look at the sea while I have 'nough money to eat. And ev after; then, nothing. Wait, we'll see. Survive, live, here. Be.

Here immob.: being part of the world; in the world. Be world. Pleasure, pleasure of being, onl of being. Observing life, mine: pulse, breathing, stomach rumblings, spitting, pissing, shitting with ease so as to feel emptied, scratch beard, see, see lots, evrthing, hear, sweat, touch, lick, be in pain, cold, too hot, wounds, sicknesses, hunger, suffering.

To die. Happy. Possible? Accept. And those from here, miserable? Accept also their misery? "Oh my dear, those adorable black kids of the tropics!" With them, without them, all alone? Fake true quandary?

All that, era lit ideas, romantic.

Here? Why not? What would I lose? My life no life in Budap?

And civ, culture, evolution, progress?

What have we done with it! Horrors, here even in Cartagena, all the slaves from Africa, six millions black Jews, horror.

I read nothing. No books, no newspapers. We are making

no one's acquaintance. Speak amg us. Vry little. S. only wants sex eat drink sun. Her roughness, her desire, her animality. No memories, childhood, future, projects, house, trips, with you, or just you, etc. Not even money. Oh. The exchange of bodies, only bodies. I love (that). But I believe there is . . . But: romant vision, old-europe. But: the truth of this body, her body, infinite sensuality, slow discovery each parcel source pleasure.

This morning, seen a very-very old black woman, crazy, pulling her enormous cart in the street in front of the hotel. Cart filled with waste, garbage, paper bags, bits of cloth, bottles. Indescribable misery. She was in rags, very dirty. She wasn't begging, spoke to herself out loud, cursing everybody, the world. We see a lot of those like her here, but I noticed her because of the immensity of her cart, barely mobile, which she dragged on the street with infinite effort. She blocked, or almost, the street, cars passed her with difficulty, honking, she insulted them non stop.

Told S.:

One day, the Great God of the Slaves, will take this old mad woman by the hand and bring her to the best restaurant in town. He will tell her: you are very tired, sit down here, rest from your life. If you're hungry, you will be served food and drink. And all the staff will wait on you hand and foot. And she will eat and drink, and the Great God of the Slaves will gently close her eyes, and He will take her up there with Him, and He will have her sit on His right. And the old woman will insult him.

To have courage for

I feel like crying all t time

I was never told. I couldn't knw it on my own. Who could have helped me? Even though I read so much. But books"

I am lying down curled up on my side in the grass in the field behind a house in Burgundy that a friend has lent us. It's spring, the beginning of spring. It's still cold, but the blue of the sky is a true blue—when I can see it in between the many passing clouds. When the sun goes into hiding, I curl up, close my eyes and wait for its reappearance. I suffer when it doesn't shine. I'm cold, it's dark—but I'm full of hope, and I only live for the nearby moment: I know that the sun, even briefly, even the timid sun of early spring, will come back, will shine on me, will warm me.

I stay lying down like an animal, with no movement, no other goal, I might even dare say without any other reason for being than the wait for this brief moment . . . delicious . . . when the sun will shine on me.

This happened a long time ago. J. was barely six years old. On second thought, much less because it was during this vacation that I filmed her with a goat that frightened her. Y. wasn't born yet. So this happened more than twenty-six years ago. But I remember this moment acutely. The tension, *the total hope* with which I awaited the sun.

My life depended on it.

*Leányfalu, Touraine, Paris,*
*January 2001–February 2002*